9/01

Down Syndrome

Down
Syndrome

by Salvatore Tocci

Franklin Watts
A DIVISION OF GROLIER PUBLISHING
New York • London • Hong Kong • Sydney
Danbury, Connecticut

Photographs ©: Monkmeyer Press: 45 (Kathleen Marie Menke/Crystal Images), 86, 128 (John MacPherson); Peter Arnold Inc.: 26 (Leonard Lessin), 115 (Matt Meadows); Photo Researchers: 21 (Eugene Gordon), 69 (Roberta Hershenson), 17, 58 (Richard Hutchings), 66 (Ken Lax), 3, 37, 99 (Ursula Markus), cover top left (Gary Parker/SPL), 53 (Elaine Rebman), cover bottom, 83, 122 (Bruce Roberts), 12 (Erika Stone), 106 (Catherine Ursillo); Photofest: 77; Photography of Brianne Treants, Courtesy of Kathy Treants: cover top right; Stock Boston: 79 (Elizabeth Crews), 103 (Stephen Frisch).

Visit Franklin Watts on the Internet at:
http://publishing.grolier.com

Interior design by
Elizabeth Helmetsie

Library of Congress Cataloging-in-Publication Data

Tocci, Salvatore.
    Down syndrome / Salvatore Tocci
        p.   cm. — (Venture)
    Includes bibliographical references and index.
    Summary: Presents the disorder known as Down Syndrome, covering such aspects as historical background, medical causes, physical and mental limitations, and development from infancy through adulthood, including sexuality, social skills, and group homes.
    ISBN 0-531-11589-5
    1. Down syndrome Juvenile literature. 2. Mental retardation Juvenile literature. [1. Down syndrome. 2. Mentally handicapped.]
I. Title. II. Series: Venture book (Franklin Watts, Inc.)
RJ506.D68T63 2000
616.85'8842—dc21   99-31019
                                              CIP

© 2000 by Franklin Watts
A division of Grolier Publishing Co., Inc.
All rights reserved. Published simultaneously in Canada
Printed in the United States of America
1 2 3 4 5 6 7 8 9 10 R 08 07 06 05 04 03 02 01 00

Contents

Michael's Story

ON A BEAUTIFUL, still, sunny day, when the sea is calm and the waves gently lap the rocks, we sit and dream about the mysterious world of the sea or we walk for miles around the Cape and along the coast. My favorite pastime is picking smooth pebbles and throwing them into the waves. I am standing on a balcony but suddenly a gust of wind blows and doors slam shut. I go inside. I am watching the black clouds roll on. It is dark and there is a streak of lightning and then a crash of thunder. I feel excited. It's like being in a movie, in a ship in a storm in the ocean.

The above passage is from an award-winning essay Michael Regos wrote while he was in ninth grade. Michael especially likes to write about places he has visited such as Bali, Kuala Lumpur, and Singapore.

Singapore is lush with tropical trees and shrubs. It is green and beautiful! It is very small, very clean, every bit of space is used as best as possible. The streets are spotless. Then as you wander among the street food courts, there is a smell! Not pleasant! The guide told us that it is a tropical fruit called "durian." It smells like public toilets, but tastes like heaven!

After reading these passages, you might think that Michael was born with a talent for writing. However, learning how to express himself was extremely difficult for Michael. In fact, he did not find it easy to learn most things. Although he said his first word at 18 months, he had trouble speaking during his early school years. Sometimes he spoke in sentences. At other times, he had trouble giving one-word answers to questions. Sometimes he initiated conversations. Some days, he was very quiet and said nothing. Yet when Michael did speak, his words and responses to questions indicated that he was quite intelligent.

Like all children, Michael could be stubborn at times. But occasionally he carried it too far. The first word he said in kindergarten was "banana." This was a word that he would say over and over both in school and at home. Michael knew that he irritated his parents by constantly saying "banana." But he just kept on saying it.

At school, Michael sat in class but he was not expected to do what other children did. At age 12, he could not read, but he spent a lot of time turning the pages of books that others in the class could read. He had the writing skills of a six-year-old. He had trouble tying his shoelaces. He also could not hold up both hands with his index fingers extended and the other fingers flexed. Michael had to use his left hand to hold down all but the index finger of his right hand.

When he was spoken to, Michael often hung down his head and pretended that he was deaf. He had very little self-confidence. He became excited and anxious when faced with a new situation. When he visited the high school he was about to enter, Michael simply lay down on the floor and refused to move. Once again, all he would say was "banana." His high school teacher was dreading Michael's arrival that fall.

As a child, Michael was given a toy called "My Talking Computer." One of the first things he typed was "I CAN READ I GET SILLY I CAN'T STOP SOMETIMES SCHOOL THINK I'M STUPID." The Christmas before he entered high school, Michael began to communicate with his family, neighbors, and friends by typing his responses on a small machine known as a communicator. He used the communicator everywhere he went. His parents said that he walked taller and had more self-confidence. Michael said that the communicator enabled him to express his thoughts and feelings when words failed him. With the use of his communicator, Michael began to show that he understood more than people had imagined he did.

In his first year in high school, Michael got a 90 percent on the final examination in German, which was a new subject for all students. A vocabulary test the next year placed Michael above the 99th percentile, confirming what others had believed—Michael had an excellent vocabulary but had trouble expressing it aloud.

What was it about Michael that made him so different from most other students his age? All of this happened to Michael because of a condition he has. Michael has Down syndrome. In this book, you will learn what Down syndrome is. You will also read about the problems and hurdles that children like Michael face. Most children with Down syndrome unfortunately do not overcome the problems and hurdles as Michael did. In fact, Michael is an exception to what usually happens as children with Down syndrome grow up. As you will read in Chapter 2, most children with Down syndrome have some degree of mental retardation and face a number of medical and social problems.

Unlike most children with Down syndrome, Michael is one of the small group of those who have developed an intelligence level that borders near the normal range. Although he may not be typical of a child who has Down syndrome, Michael represents what all children with Down syndrome want—to be as normal as possible. As Michael has put it, "I'm trying to live like a human being, not a person with Down syndrome."

CHAPTER 2

Down Syndrome

IN THE 1860s, John Langdon Down, a British doctor, had been observing a large number of children who were mentally retarded. Some of these children had severe mental retardation, others were moderately retarded, and still others displayed only mild mental retardation. But what struck Dr. Down was what all these children had in common. He noticed the physical features that most of them shared.

In a medical journal published in 1866, Dr. Down wrote "[Their] hair is . . . of a brownish colour, straight and scanty. The face is flat and broad. The cheeks are roundish. The eyes are obliquely placed. The forehead is wrinkled. The lips are large and thick. The tongue is long, thick, and is much roughened. The nose is small. The skin has a slightly

. . . yellowish tinge, and [gives] the appearance of being too large for the body."

Dr. Down was the first to describe the features that are typical of people with a condition which is known today as *Down syndrome*. A *syndrome* is a collection of features or symptoms that characterize or indicate a disease or some abnormal condition. Because Dr. Down was the first to record the features in these children, the syndrome bears his name. Down syndrome is an abnormal condition marked by some degree of mental retardation and certain distinct physical features.

Today, Down syndrome is recognized as one of the most common birth defects. It occurs in all races, ethnic groups, socioeconomic classes, and nationalities. It can happen to anyone and occurs equally in boys and girls. One in every 800 to 1,000 children is born with Down syndrome. Approximately 5,500 children with Down syndrome are born each year in the United States alone. Nearly 250,000 families in the United States have a child with Down syndrome.

Physical Features

As Dr. Down first reported, people with Down syndrome often possess certain physical features. Most of these features, especially those in the face, are apparent at an early age—even at birth. In fact, doctors are often able to diagnose Down syndrome in a newborn solely on the basis of these features. Additional tests can then be ordered to confirm the diagnosis.

One facial feature present in a child with Down syndrome is a broad or flat face. Such children often have an unusually small nose. The nasal passages may also be smaller and, as

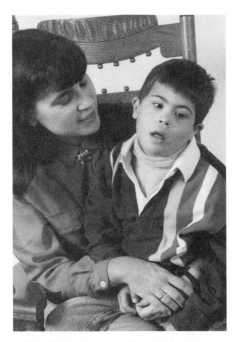

The facial features shared by children with Down syndrome are obvious.

a result, they can become congested more easily. The child's eyes often appear to slant upward. Because of the Asian appearance caused by these slanted eyes, Down syndrome was once called "mongolism." In fact, Dr. Down referred to the "Mongolian type" in the paper he wrote in 1866.

A child with Down syndrome may also have small folds of skin known as *epicanthic folds* at the inner corners of the eyes. The outer part of the iris—the colored part of the eye—may have light spots called Brushfield spots. However, such spots are more common in Down syndrome children with blue eyes. These spots are not very noticeable and do not affect the child's vision. Other facial features include a smaller mouth and ears that have an abnormal shape. In some cases, the ears may be located slightly lower on the head, and their tops may fold over.

Partly because of the smaller size of the mouth, the tongue often appears to be larger than normal. The teeth are also affected in children with Down syndrome. Most babies get their teeth in a regular sequence, but those with Down syndrome may get their teeth in a random order. In addition, their teeth may be small, have unusual shapes, and be out of place. These problems may continue when these children get their permanent teeth later in life.

With a smaller nose, mouth, and ears, it is not surprising that children with Down syndrome have smaller than normal heads. Their head size usually falls within the lowest 3 percent on standard growth charts for children. But because their body size is also smaller than normal, their smaller head size is not noticeable. In fact, their head size is within a normal range relative to their body size. The back of the head of a child with Down syndrome may be flatter and the neck is usually shorter. At birth, a loose fold of skin may be present on each side of the neck. These skin folds tend to disappear as the child gets older.

The hands of a child with Down syndrome are often smaller, and the fingers may be shorter. The fifth finger may curve inward slightly, having only one crease rather than the normal two. Similarly, the palm of the hand often has only a single deep crease extending across the center. The feet are usually normal in both size and shape, but the space between the first and second toe may be quite large. The skin may be fair and have a spotted appearance. Children with Down syndrome usually have less hair than normal, and the hair may also be thin and soft.

Muscle Tone

Our muscles can contract or relax, but muscles never relax completely. They remain in a state of partial contraction. This condition is referred to as *muscle tone*. People with Down syndrome have low muscle tone. In a newborn baby, the presence of low muscle tone will alert a doctor to look for other signs of Down syndrome.

13

As a result of low muscle tone, the muscles are more relaxed than normal, giving them a "floppy" appearance. The muscles are also more difficult to control. For example, the tongue with its relatively large size may uncontrollably protrude from the mouth. Low muscle tone affects not only the tongue but the muscles throughout the body. As a result, a baby with Down syndrome will have a harder time learning to sit upright, stand, and walk. Eating can also be difficult as the muscles of the mouth do not function normally in accepting and chewing solid food. Low muscle tone cannot be cured but it may improve over time. Physical therapy can also improve it so that people with Down syndrome can function more normally.

Not all children with Down syndrome will have all these physical traits. One child with Down syndrome might have only a few of these traits, while another child might have many. But three physical features are likely to be present in a child with Down syndrome: low muscle tone, upward-slanted eyes, and small ears. Another trait shared by almost all people with Down syndrome is a lower-than-normal intelligence.

Intelligence

For many years, standardized tests have been used to measure intelligence. You have probably taken one of these standardized tests in school. Such tests are designed to measure a person's intelligence quotient (IQ). A person's IQ reflects that individual's ability to think, reason, solve problems, interpret meanings, and form ideas.

With an IQ range between 70 and 130, 95 percent of the population is considered to be of "normal" intelligence.

Anyone with an IQ over 130 is considered to have "superi-or" intelligence. Such people make up 2.5 percent of the population. The remaining 2.5 percent have an IQ below 70 and are considered as having mental retardation.

The lower the IQ, the more mentally retarded the individual. A person with an IQ between 55 and 69 is considered to have mild mental retardation. Anyone with an IQ between 40 and 54 is considered to have moderate mental retardation. Anyone with an IQ between 25 and 39 is said to have severe mental retardation. Most children with Down syndrome have IQs that fall between 40 and 69, indicating moderate to mild mental retardation. Some children have IQs below 40, indicating severe mental retardation. On the other hand, some children with Down syndrome have IQs that place them near the normal range.

Because of their lower-than-normal IQs, children with Down syndrome were mistreated for many years. Such children were considered to be incapable of learning and were often placed in institutions. Separated from society, these children were given little or no education. People usually ignored them and made no effort to stimulate their minds. In such a deprived environment, these children could never hope to grow intellectually. Rather, they merely fulfilled the low expectations that people had for them.

Ironically, Dr. Down was somewhat responsible for the mistreatment that children with Down syndrome experienced. In the paper he wrote, Dr. Down referred to the children he had examined as "idiots" because of their below-normal intelligence. An idiot is a person who has severe mental retardation with an IQ between 25 and 39. Many children with Down syndrome have higher IQs, but unfortunately Dr. Down's label stuck, along with another term he used—"Mongolian." As a result, people with Down syndrome became known as "Mongoloid idiots," a term that has long been discarded. Today, people recognize that Down syndrome is not an indication that a person is severely mentally retarded, inferior, unhappy, or unable to function in society.

Role in Society

Some experts feel that the number of people with Down syndrome will double in the next ten years. The main reason for this increase is the change in how society reacts to people with Down syndrome. No longer hidden away in institutions, children with Down syndrome have become increasingly integrated in our society. They are actively involved in community organizations, such as schools, workforces, health care systems, and social and recreational activities. Their involvement in society has resulted in a more stimulating environment for children with Down syndrome. As a result, their development—intellectually, physically, emotionally, and socially—has dramatically increased. Today, people with Down syndrome are functioning at increasingly higher skill levels.

As an integral part of society, people with Down syndrome can now benefit from advances in medical technology. In 1910, some 40 years after Dr. Down wrote his paper, children with Down syndrome were expected to survive only to age 9. In the 1940s, when antibiotics became available, their life expectancy increased to 20. Today, with advances in medical technology and clinical treatments, nearly 80 percent of adults with Down syndrome live to be

*Special Olympics events give children with Down syndrome a sense
of pride and achievement.*

55, and many live even longer. As their life expectancy
increases, more and more people with Down syndrome will
find their place in society.

Obviously, it is important for society—you—to have an
attitude that allows people with Down syndrome to feel
accepted and involved. They should be given the same
rights and privileges as anyone else and be treated with the
same respect. But, unfortunately, not everyone has reacted
to people with Down syndrome in a caring and understanding manner. Like those with other disabilities, people
with Down syndrome have often faced prejudice and discrimination. In response, the United States Congress has
passed several laws to ensure that anyone with a disability

such as Down syndrome has the right to live and work in the community to the fullest extent possible.

Anti-Discrimination Laws

In 1973, Congress passed the Rehabilitation Act. Two years later, Congress passed the Individuals with Disabilities Education Act (IDEA). In 1990, it placed into law the Americans with Disabilities Act (ADA). These three laws prohibit discrimination against people with disabilities, including Down syndrome.

The Rehabilitation Act prohibits discrimination against disabled people in federally funded programs. The law states that "No otherwise qualified individual with handicaps in the United States . . . shall, solely by reason of his handicap, be excluded from the participation in, be denied the benefits of, or be subjected to discrimination under any program or activity receiving federal financial assistance . . ." The U.S. Supreme Court has ruled that an "otherwise qualified" handicapped individual is one who is "able to meet all of the program's requirements in spite of his handicap." The programs that receive federal financial assistance include schools. Thus a child with Down syndrome, or any other disability, is legally entitled to attend the local school.

In 1975, Congress strengthened the Rehabilitation Act by passing the Individuals with Disabilities Education Act (IDEA). Under the IDEA, the federal government provides funds for the education of children with disabilities to each state that has a special education program that meets federal standards. States that accept federal funds under the IDEA must provide both approved educational services and a variety of rights to children with disabilities—and to their parents. States can create educational services that are better than those required by the IDEA, and some states have done so.

The IDEA states that every part of a disabled child's special education program at school must be provided at public expense. In other words, the family of the child with the disability is not responsible for paying any part of the cost of educating their child. If the public school does not have a suitable special education program, the school must place the child in a private program and pay the full cost.

The IDEA requires that the program meet the unique needs of a child with a disability. This may require special education teachers, physical therapists, social workers, and any other supportive staff necessary to enable the child to benefit from the program. The law also states that the child should have as much contact as possible with children who do not have disabilities. This provision is aimed at making sure that schools do not segregate children with disabilities, as they were once segregated in institutions. Many children with Down syndrome attend regular classes, going to a separate room only for their special needs, such as physical therapy. Children with Down syndrome who cannot attend regular classes may join their classmates for certain activities such as lunch, plays, and assemblies.

The IDEA requires states to provide special education services for children between 3 and 18 years old. If a state offers public education to any student up to the age of 21, then it must also provide special education services to children with disabilities up to the same age. In 1986, Congress passed a law that provides grants to states that create an approved program to include infants with disabilities from birth to 2 years old. Some form of this service for infants is available in every state.

According to the IDEA, every child with a disability must be evaluated by professionals. Each state must develop testing and evaluation procedures designed to identify the abilities and needs of each child before that child is placed in a special education program. For a child with Down syndrome, the process is simple and straightforward. Almost all school districts recognize that a child with Down syndrome needs some form of special education services.

The testing and evaluation of each child with a disability results in the development of an Individualized Education Plan (IEP). A child's IEP is usually created through a series of meetings involving teachers, counselors, parents, and perhaps even the child. The IEP describes the child's present level of development, the goals of the special education services, the specific services the child will receive, and the extent to which the child will participate in regular education programs. The IEP also indicates when the special services will start and how long they will last. Most importantly, the IEP includes standards to measure the success of the special education services.

The Americans with Disabilities Act (ADA) of 1990 states that private employers cannot discriminate against employees or people seeking a job who have a disability. This law does not require an employer to hire someone with a disability, but the employer cannot refuse to hire a qualified person simply because of his or her disability. Another section of this law applies to public facilities. The ADA prohibits discrimination against people with disabilities in such public facilities as hotels, motels, theaters, restaurants, stadiums, concert halls, grocery stores, museums, libraries, bowling alleys, senior citizen centers, gas stations, department stores, airport terminals, train stations, and zoos.

None of these facilities may exclude a person with a disability such as Down syndrome from a regularly scheduled program. In addition, they cannot restrict disabled people to certain times or days and cannot offer them a special

Some people with Down syndrome may not be able to walk due to a medical problem.

program in place of a regular one. The only exception is if the event organizer can show that admitting a person with a disability to the regular program would result in an unreasonable expense.

To accommodate people with disabilities, existing public facilities have had to make a number of changes. Facilities built since the ADA was passed have taken the law's requirements into consideration in the designing stages. Overall, the ADA has been responsible for major changes in public facilities. What's more important is the fact that the ADA, along with the Rehabilitation Act and the Individuals with Disabilities Education Act, has been responsible for major changes in people's lives. Consider the impact it has had on Jason Kingsley's and Mitchell Levitz's lives. Both Jason and Mitchell have overcome many of the obstacles that confront children with Down syndrome.

Jason and Mitchell

Shortly after he was born, Jason's parents were told that he had Down syndrome. The doctor recommended that Jason be placed in an institution, but his parents decided to ignore that advice. Instead, they brought Jason home and, because of the IDEA, were able to enroll him in both pre-school and public school. When he was only 15 months old, Jason appeared on "Sesame Street," the first child with Down syndrome to appear on that show. By age 4, Jason was able to read. By age 7, he could count to 10 in 12 languages. When he was 10, Jason played a role on a network television program.

Mitchell's parents, too, were told to place their child in an institution shortly after he was born with Down syndrome. But, like Jason, Mitchell was raised at home. Because of the IDEA, Mitchell also attended a local school and graduated with a regular diploma when he was 18. In addition, he received awards for community service and academic achievement in business education, as well as a varsity letter for soccer. Mitchell has also made several appearances on network television, including talk shows.

Jason and Mitchell met each other at the preschool they attended, and as they grew up, they remained friends. In 1994, a book they wrote together was published. Their book, *Count Us In,* describes the boys' thoughts and feelings on a wide range of subjects, including their experiences growing up with Down syndrome. Today, their book is read by parents and teachers of children with Down syndrome. In addition, *Count Us In* is used as a college text and as a professional medical reference book. Despite their disability, Jason and Mitchell have shown what some people with Down syndrome can accomplish, given the opportunities.

CHAPTER 3

Causes of Down Syndrome

OWN SYNDROME is a birth defect, and to understand what a birth defect is, you must first know something about *genetics*. Genetics is the study of heredity, or how traits are passed from parents to their offspring. Some of the traits you inherited are quite obvious to anyone. Such traits include the color of your eyes, the length of your fingers, the thickness of your hair, and the size of your head. Other traits that you inherited from your parents are not so obvious. These include your ability to see colors, detect odors, and identify sounds. And some of the traits you inherited are not visible at all to others—or even to you. These include your ability to digest milk, the level of sugar that circulates in your blood, and your blood type.

Genes

All these traits are controlled by genes. A *gene* is the basic unit of heredity. Think of a gene as a blueprint or a set of computer instructions. If the blueprint has been drawn correctly, then the builder should not make any mistakes. If the computer instructions have been written correctly, then the program should operate smoothly. But if an error has been made in the blueprint, the builder might leave out a window, for example. If an error has been made in the computer program, the program might crash.

The same is true of genes. If genes are correctly formed, the traits will be normal. True, there will be a range or variety. One person may be 5 feet 2 inches (157 centimeters), while someone else may be 6 feet 7 inches (201 cm). Someone will have light blue eyes, while someone else will have dark brown eyes. Someone might hear a pin drop, while someone else will need to turn up the volume on the radio. But if there is an error in the genes, then a person might be 8 feet (244 cm) tall, have no color in his or her eyes, or be unable to hear anything.

Chromosomes

Scientists knew about genes and their role in heredity long before they learned where genes are in a person's cells. A *cell* is the building block of your body. In fact, your body has more than 100 trillion (100,000,000,000,000) cells. Each of these cells contains the genes, or blueprints, needed to perform its job correctly. But where exactly are the genes inside each cell?

Scientists finally figured out that the genes are located on the chromosomes. A *chromosome* is a microscopic, rod-

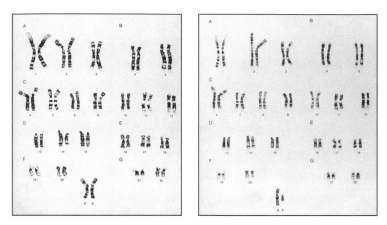

A karyotype of a normal human female (left). A karyotype of a normal human male (right).

shaped body inside the cell. Each cell of your body, with a few exceptions, contains 46 chromosomes. Chromosomes come in pairs—23 pairs in each cell. A picture of all the chromosomes in a single cell is called a *karyotype.* To produce a karyotype, the cells are grown or cultured in small containers known as petri dishes. At a certain point, the cells are broken open. The chromosomes are removed, collected, and photographed under a microscope. The photograph is then cut to separate each chromosome. The chromosomes are then paired to prepare the karyotype.

The karyotype shown above on the left displays the chromosomes from the cell of a female. The members of each pair of chromosomes have a similar structure. The pairs are numbered from 1 to 22. One pair is not numbered but is labeled as XX. These are the *sex chromosomes.* The sex chromosomes determine the sex of an individual and this pair of sex chromosomes—XX—results in a female.

The karyotype shown above on the right is from a male. The chromosomes are again arranged in pairs and numbered from 1 to 22. But in males, only the members of these 22 pairs have a similar structure. Unlike the situation in females, the members of the 23rd pair—the sex chromosomes—do not have a similar structure. Notice that they are labeled XY. The XY chromosome pair results in a male.

Cell Divisions

When a cell divides to form two new cells, each new cell must receive a complete set—all 23 pairs—of chromosomes. If a cell does not receive a complete set, it will be missing some of its genetic "blueprints" and thus will not be able to function normally. There are two ways in which cells divide. One way is known as *mitosis*.

Mitosis is the process by which all cells—except the reproductive cells—divide. The reproductive cells include sperm and eggs. A cell that undergoes mitosis is called a *parent cell*. Before mitosis begins, a parent cell duplicates—makes copies of—its chromosomes. At this point, the cell has two copies of each pair of chromosomes—or 46 pairs. As the parent cell divides during mitosis, a copy of each pair of chromosomes passes into each of the two cells that are produced. The two cells produced by mitosis are called *daughter cells*. Each daughter cell has the same number and kinds of chromosomes as the parent cell had.

When scientists understood what happens during mitosis, they predicted that a different process should occur in reproductive cells. These reproductive cells will divide to produce either mature sperm or egg cells. The scientists reasoned that if mitosis produced mature sperm and eggs, then each reproductive cell would contain 23 pairs, or 46 chromosomes. So if a sperm fertilized an egg, the result would be a total of 92 chromosomes. The presence of one extra chromosome can create problems. A human cell with 92 chromosomes could never survive. The researchers knew there had to be a second type of cell division for sperm and eggs, in which each would receive half of the chromosomes, or only 23 chromosomes. Then when fertilization took place, the 23 chromosomes in the sperm would combine with the 23 chromosomes in the egg for a total of 46 chromosomes—the normal number in a human cell. Scientists discovered this type of cell division, known as *meiosis.*

Meiosis is the process of cell division that results in the production of sperm and eggs that can participate in fertilization. Meiosis begins like mitosis with the duplication of each chromosome. However, in meiosis, the events that follow are more complicated. In fact, meiosis involves two divisions that result in four cells rather than one division like mitosis. But to understand what causes Down syndrome, all you need to know about meiosis is that, normally, each member of a pair of chromosomes splits or disjoins from the other. This process is called *disjunction.*

As a result of disjunction, each cell produced by meiosis gets only one chromosome from the original pair. Thus each sperm and egg contains only 23 chromosomes, half the usual number. At fertilization, the 23 chromosomes in the sperm unite with the 23 chromosomes in the egg to make the normal number—46.

Abnormal Cell Divisions

Not every cell division occurs normally, however. In fact, errors involving the chromosomes are common. For example, chromosomes may not duplicate correctly. And, parts of chromosomes may get lost as a cell divides. Even an entire chromosome may fail to pass into a newly formed cell. On the other hand, the cell may receive too many chromosomes.

If the error involving the chromosomes occurs during mitosis, the consequences may not even be noticeable. For example, the error may occur in a skin cell that is undergoing mitosis. The error may prevent the cell from functioning normally or even result in the death of the cell. But, other skin cells can undergo mitosis to replace any that died. In some cases, however, mistakes that occur during mitosis may have serious consequences. For example, if mitosis is not kept under control, cell divisions will continue. Masses of cells will be produced, leading to the formation of tumors. Thus, mitosis that is out of control may result in a cancer.

If an error involving the chromosomes occurs during meiosis, the consequences can also be quite serious. Since meiosis produces mature sperm and eggs that can participate in fertilization, an error that occurs during meiosis may lead to a reproductive cell with abnormal chromosomes. If this abnormal reproductive cell participates in fertilization, the fertilized egg will contain a chromosome abnormality. The fertilized egg may fail to develop because of the chromosome abnormality. Even if it does develop, it often fails to develop fully—the pregnant woman may suffer a miscarriage. A *miscarriage* is a pregnancy that ends because of some natural cause. More than half of all miscarriages during the first three months of pregnancy are due to a chromosome abnormality in the fertilized egg.

If a fertilized egg with a chromosome abnormality develops fully, chances are that the child will have some type of abnormal condition. Soon after fertilization, the fertilized egg begins to divide by mitosis. Mitosis continues until there are trillions of cells. Each daughter cell produced by mitosis contains the same number and kinds of chromosomes as its parent cell, so every cell in the child's body will have the same chromosome abnormality that was present in the fertilized egg. Such is the case with 99 percent of the children born with Down syndrome.

Trisomy 21

Most cases of Down syndrome are caused by the failure of chromosomes to separate properly during meiosis. During disjunction, each reproductive cell should receive only one chromosome from the original pair. But occasionally the chromosomes do not separate properly. This is referred to as *nondisjunction.* As a result of nondisjunction, one reproductive cell may receive 24 chromosomes while another reproductive cell may receive 22 chromosomes. The cell with 22 chromosomes will not survive. But the one with 24 chromosomes will survive, even though it has one extra chromosome.

If the reproductive cell with 24 chromosomes fertilizes a normal reproductive cell with 23 chromosomes, then the fertilized egg will contain 47 chromosomes. In this case, the fertilized egg will contain an extra copy—for a total of three copies of a chromosome instead of the normal pair. This condition is called *trisomy,* which means "three chromosomes." In Down syndrome, it is chromosome number 21 that does not separate properly during meiosis. One reproductive cell does not receive a chromosome 21, while another receives both copies. If the reproductive cell that has both copies of chromosome 21 unites during fertilization with a normal reproductive cell that has one copy of chromosome 21, then the fertilized egg will have three copies of chromosome 21. This condition is known as *trisomy 21*—another term for Down syndrome. Approximately 95 percent of Down syndrome cases are the result of trisomy 21 caused by nondisjunction.

In trisomy 21, the extra chromosome 21 in the fertilized egg will be copied and passed into each new cell that is produced by mitosis. As a result, all the child's cells will contain three copies of chromosome 21.

Exactly why three copies of chromosome 21 result in Down syndrome is not known. However, scientists do know that the extra chromosome 21 results in a cell that is more active than a normal cell. The genes on the chromosomes are responsible for making a class of chemical compounds known as *proteins*. Having an extra chromosome means more genes are present, and having more genes means that more proteins are made. Researchers are trying to find out exactly what kinds of proteins are made and what they do in the cell.

Scientists also do not know why a chromosome 21 pair fails to separate properly during meiosis. This nondisjunction may occur when either a sperm or egg is produced. However, 85 to 90 percent of babies born with Down syndrome developed from an egg that contained an extra chromosome 21. Nondisjunction is more likely to occur during meiosis in a female who produces egg cells than in a male who produces sperm cells. Only 10 to 15 percent of babies born with Down syndrome developed from a nondisjunction that occurred when a sperm was produced.

Nondisjunction occurs more often in females than males because a female is born with all the eggs she will ever have.

She does not produce new eggs during her lifetime. The process of meiosis starts in a female's eggs even before she herself is born. The eggs do not complete the meiosis process, however. They stop at some point during the division. Only when the female reaches puberty will she have the hormones that are needed by the eggs to complete meiosis. Even then, only one egg cell will complete the process every 28 days. Thus an egg cell may remain suspended in meiosis for years, or even for decades. During that time, something may happen to cause the chromosomes to become "sticky." Then they will not be able to separate properly when meiosis starts up again.

The longer the egg remains suspended in meiosis, the more likely the chromosomes are to stick together when they attempt to move apart. That is why nondisjunction is more likely to occur as a woman gets older. This theory is confirmed by looking at the chances of a woman having a baby with Down syndrome as she gets older. In women under the age of 30, the incidence of Down syndrome is less than 1 in 1,000 births. However, in women just 10 years older—40—the chances of having a child with Down syndrome are ten times greater—1 in 105 births. In another 8 years—48—the incidence increases to 1 in 12 births. Age is not a factor with men because a male produces new sperm cells throughout his reproductive life. The sperm are not stored in a state of partial meiosis, and thus the chromosomes do not have as much time to become "sticky."

Other Causes

Approximately 95 percent of the children with Down syndrome are the result of nondisjunction resulting in trisomy

21, but what about the remaining 5 percent? Two other errors involving the chromosomes may lead to Down syndrome. One takes place during meiosis; the other occurs during mitosis.

What happens in meiosis is known as a *translocation*. A translocation involves taking a part of a chromosome and sticking it on another chromosome. As in nondisjunction, there is an extra chromosome 21. But in translocation, this extra chromosome 21 does not remain separate. Instead, a part of it breaks off and becomes attached to another chromosome, usually number 14. Translocation between chromosomes 21 and 14 accounts for approximately 4 percent of Down syndrome cases.

In the remaining 1 percent, children with Down syndrome are the result of *mosaicism*. In mosaicism, all the cells in an individual do not have the same number of chromosomes. Mosaicism occurs when nondisjunction of chromosome 21 takes place in one of the cells that developed by mitosis from the fertilized egg. This results in a mixture of two types of cells. The cells produced by the mitosis of normal cells have 46 chromosomes. The cells produced by the mitosis of cells with an extra chromosome number 21 have 47 chromosomes. The individual is thus a "mosaic," having a mixture of two types of cells.

Detecting Down Syndrome

Because Down syndrome is caused by an event that occurs very early in life, it is possible to detect this condition at some point before birth. Four different tests are available to check an unborn baby, or *fetus,* for Down syndrome. Two of these tests are diagnostic—they give a definite answer as to whether or not the fetus has Down syndrome.

One such test is known as *amniocentesis,* which is generally performed between 14 and 18 weeks after pregnancy begins. In amniocentesis, a long thin needle is inserted through the mother's belly into the womb. Before this procedure, pictures are taken to determine the location and size of the fetus. The needle is then carefully manipulated to avoid the fetus. The needle is used to withdraw some of the fluid that surrounds the fetus. This fluid contains some cells shed by the fetus. A karyotype is prepared and examined for any chromosome abnormality that would indicate Down syndrome.

Another diagnostic test is *chorionic villus sampling (CVS).* CVS can be performed earlier than amniocentesis, between the 9th and 12th week of pregnancy. In this procedure, samples that include cells are taken from a part of the womb that helps nourish the fetus but that is not part of the fetus itself. Again, a karyotype is prepared to check for Down syndrome.

Two other tests, known as screening tests, may or may not reveal the presence of Down syndrome in a fetus. Both these tests screen the mother's blood. One test measures the level of a certain protein, known as alpha fetoprotein. A low level of this protein is associated with Down syndrome. The other blood test measures the level of three chemical substances in the mother's blood. The results are evaluated to estimate the risk of having a child with Down syndrome. If either of these two screening tests indicate that the fetus may have Down syndrome, the mother may want to undergo one of the diagnostic tests to confirm that possibility.

Future Babies

Parents of a child with Down syndrome always ask their doctor about the odds of having another child with the same condition. The answer depends on what caused Down syndrome in their child. In cases caused by translocation, one of the parents may have the translocation as part of his or her genetic makeup, and the child may inherit this translocation. The risk of having another child with Down syndrome in this case can be as high as 100 percent or as low as 2 percent. Several factors affect the risk, including the sex of the parent with the translocation. Parents of a child with Down syndrome caused by translocation should have their karyotypes prepared. Then they should consult with a doctor to discuss their chances of having another child with Down syndrome.

The situation is different in the case of parents of a child with Down syndrome caused by nondisjunction. In this case, the chance of having another child with Down syndrome is approximately 1 percent—1 in 100 births—regardless of the mother's age. This represents a larger than normal risk for women under 30, for whom the incidence of having a child with Down syndrome is usually less than 1 in 1,000 births. But in spite of the increased risk, many parents of a child with Down syndrome caused by nondisjunction have decided to have more children. And, as the odds predicted, most of these children did not have Down syndrome.

CHAPTER 4

Infancy

Y OU MAY THINK that a baby with Down syndrome will not grow up healthy and active, but this is not necessarily the case. In fact, babies born with Down syndrome can be just as healthy and active as other children. However, infants with Down syndrome do face a greater likelihood of developing certain medical problems. Some of these problems can be serious or even life-threatening. Fortunately, most of them can be treated if they are detected early enough.

Not every child with Down syndrome has the physical features that were described in Chapter 2. Similarly, not every infant with Down syndrome has the medical problems discussed in this chapter. Some children will have no problems. Others will have a few problems. Unfortunately, some will

A baby with Down syndrome and her mom enjoy a playful moment.

have many of the medical conditions discussed in this chapter. If a baby is born with a medical problem, the parents will be advised as to how to care for their child. The parents will also be informed about symptoms that might indicate a medical problem. Should a problem develop, immediate medical attention and parental care can often correct it.

Circulatory Problems

The circulatory system consists of the heart, blood vessels, and blood. Babies with Down syndrome may have a problem with any one of these. A defect present at birth is known as a *congenital defect*. About 40 to 45 percent of babies with Down syndrome are born with a congenital heart defect. Before examining the congenital heart defects that babies with Down syndrome may have, you must first understand how the heart functions.

Your heart is a muscular structure about the size of your fist. Like any other muscle, your heart can contract and relax. As it contracts and relaxes, it pumps blood throughout the body. To carry out its job, the heart is divided into a left side and right side. Each side contains two chambers, for a total of four chambers.

The upper two chambers are the *atria* (singular, *atrium*). The lower two chambers are the *ventricles*. A thin wall of muscle, known as a septum, separates the left side of the heart from the right side. In addition, each atrium is separated from the ventricle beneath it by a *valve*. A valve is a flap that keeps blood flowing in the correct direction. The right atrium receives blood that is returning from all parts of the body, except the lungs. This blood contains little oxygen and much carbon dioxide. When the right atrium contracts, a valve is opened, and blood is pumped into the right ventricle. When the right ventricle contracts, the valve is shut, and blood is pumped to the lungs.

In the lungs, the blood gives off carbon dioxide and picks up oxygen. The blood then returns to the left atrium of the heart. The two atria contract at the same time. The right atrium pumps blood into the right ventricle. When the left atrium contracts, a valve opens, and blood is pumped into the left ventricle. The two ventricles contract at the same time. The right ventricle pumps blood to the lungs. When the left ventricle contracts, blood is pumped to all parts of the body except the lungs. The blood then returns to the right atrium to begin the cycle again.

Babies with Down syndrome may have several kinds of heart defects. The most common is known as *atrioventricular septal defect*, or simply AV canal. This condition is caused by a failure of the septum to close properly. The result is usually a large opening, or canal, in the center of the heart, between either the two atria or the two ventricles. In addition, the valves in the heart may be abnormal. If a valve is defective, blood will not flow correctly. If the hole appears in the septum, blood from both sides of the heart can mix. Blood low in oxygen on the right side will mix with blood rich in oxygen on the left side. So the blood being pumped out of the left ventricle will not contain as much oxygen as it should. To make up for this, the heart is forced to pump extra blood to the lungs to pick up more oxygen. In time, this extra effort causes the heart to become larger.

Another congenital heart defect is a hole that is smaller than the one associated with AV canal. All fetuses develop with a hole in the septum. In a fetus, the lungs are not working and thus cannot supply oxygen. The hole in the heart of a fetus allows the blood to flow mainly out of the left ventricle. From here the blood travels to the umbilical cord where it picks up oxygen from the mother's blood. At birth, the lungs begin to function to supply oxygen to the blood. Normally, the hole in the septum closes before a baby is born so that blood flow to the lungs is increased. But in a baby with Down syndrome, the hole often remains open. Then, blood from both sides of the heart will mix, leading to the same problems caused by AV canal.

Obviously, a congenital heart defect can be quite serious. Infants with such a defect usually need to avoid vigorous activities. They also have less stamina than other infants and get tired more easily. Because of the low oxygen content in their blood, these children sometimes develop bluish lips and fingertips. Blood with a low oxygen content has a bluish color rather than the bright red color it has when the oxygen content is normal. Many babies with Down syndrome and congenital heart defects require medication to keep their hearts functioning normally.

Fortunately, advances in medical technology have enabled doctors to correct many heart defects, including those associated with Down syndrome. For example, open-heart surgery can be performed to repair a hole that is a result of AV canal. However, such surgery must be performed before the defect has caused any permanent damage to the heart. For this reason, every baby born with Down syndrome must be carefully examined by a doctor for a possible heart defect. Most heart defects can be detected at birth. Some, however, cannot be detected until the child is a few weeks or months old.

The easiest way to detect a heart defect is with the help of an echocardiogram. An echocardiogram uses high-frequency sound waves to create a picture of the heart. Then, if a heart defect is detected, the doctor may order an X ray of the heart or an electrocardiogram. An electrocardiogram records the electrical activity of the heart, indicating how well the heart is functioning. A surgeon may also insert a probe to view the inside of the heart. This procedure is done only when serious abnormalities are suspected or the baby is about to have open-heart surgery.

The decision to perform open-heart surgery depends on a number of factors, including the seriousness of the defect and the general health of the baby. A baby with a serious AV canal may be operated on early in the first year of life. A baby with a minor hole between the ventricles may be operated on a few years after birth. Approximately 75 percent of those with serious AV canal defects can engage in normal activities following surgery. The percentage is even higher for those with less serious congenital heart defects.

Problems can also develop in the blood of babies with Down syndrome. These infants are 15 to 20 times more likely to develop *leukemia* than other children. Leukemia is a cancer of the blood. Blood contains both red blood cells, which transport oxygen, and a variety of white blood cells, which help fight infections. In leukemia, one of the white blood cell types divides uncontrollably. In most cases of leukemia in infants, a specific type of white blood cell is involved. This leukemia tends to occur within the first three years of life and fortunately, there is a high cure rate.

Digestive Problems

Approximately 10 percent of the babies born with Down syndrome have a congenital defect in their digestive system. The most common defect is a blockage or narrowing of the small intestine, which can prevent food from passing through the intestine. Another digestive problem that may arise in babies with Down syndrome is an opening that forms between the *trachea* or windpipe, and the *esophagus*, or food passage. Normally, these two passageways are separate, preventing food from passing from the mouth into the trachea, which would cause choking.

Both these digestive problems usually become apparent soon after birth. Symptoms that might indicate a blocked intestine include poor feeding, repeated vomiting, and a swollen belly. Surgery can be performed to open the blockage in the small intestine or to close the hole between the trachea and esophagus, so that babies with these conditions will be able to eat and digest foods normally.

Respiratory Problems

Before antibiotics were available, one of the most common problems in babies with Down syndrome involved the respiratory system. Such problems included *bronchitis,* which is an inflammation of the tubes that lead from the trachea to the lungs. Another common problem was *pneumonia,* which is an infection of the lungs. Today, both these problems can be easily treated with antibiotics.

However, some respiratory problems are not so easily resolved. One such problem is *sleep apnea*—temporary stoppage of breathing. In babies with Down syndrome, sleep apnea is usually caused by an obstruction in a respiratory passageway. Symptoms of this condition include snoring and a restless sleep pattern with irregular periods of wakefulness. The tongue of a baby with Down syndrome is relatively larger than its small mouth. This larger tongue may block the passage of air into the trachea, leading to sleep apnea. Larger than normal adenoids may also cause sleep apnea. An *adenoid* is a small mass of cells at the back of the throat. If enlarged adenoids are the cause, their removal can correct the problem.

Hearing Problems

About 50 percent of the babies born with Down syndrome develop hearing loss. This hearing loss may be mild, causing the infant to miss only certain sounds. Or the loss may be significant, causing the infant to miss most sounds. The ability to develop speech and language depends on hearing. With a reduced hearing capacity, an infant with Down syndrome may not be able to form sounds and words as early in life as other children.

Beginning in the second year of life, speech and language become increasingly more important in intelligence tests. Two-year-old infants with Down syndrome may show a decline in intelligence because of their delayed development of speech and language. However, some research studies have shown that early intervention can help. Several studies have tested children with Down syndrome who entered special programs as infants. These studies have found that these children performed better on a variety of tests and tasks than children with Down syndrome who were not in such programs.

The most common cause of hearing loss in infants with Down syndrome is fluid that collects in the middle ear. Sound is transmitted from the outer ear to the middle ear, and then to the inner ear. When stimulated by a sound, tiny hairs in the inner ear vibrate. These vibrations send messages to the brain that are interpreted as sounds. But fluid in the middle ear blocks sounds from reaching the inner ear so the messages are not sent from the inner ear to the brain.

Normally, any fluid that collects in the middle ear drains to the back of the throat through the eustachian tube. The *eustachian tube* is a passageway that leads from the middle ear to the throat. In an infant with Down syndrome, the eustachian tube is often blocked and as a result, fluid collects in the middle ear. This fluid not only results in hearing loss but can also serve as a site of infection. The infection may cause the hearing loss to be even more significant.

In such cases, antibiotics and decongestants can be used to treat the infection and open the passageway. If such infections occur frequently, the doctor can place small tubes through the eardrum to help drain the fluid that collects in the middle ear. Implanting these tubes is a relatively simple procedure that can be done in a doctor's office.

Infants with Down syndrome should have their hearing tested once a year. Because they often have small ear canals, these infants may need to be taken to a specialist who has the necessary medical instruments. If the specialist detects a hearing loss, the parents may be given training in how to better communicate with their child. If the hearing loss is persistent, a hearing aid may be recommended. Hearing aids are usually effective in helping to restore hearing. With early intervention, proper medical treatment, and parental involvement, an infant with Down syndrome who has a hearing problem should be able to hear well enough to develop communication skills.

Vision Problems

Nearly 70 percent of infants with Down syndrome have some type of problem with their eyes. The vision problems they have are the same as those of other children. However, the chances of an infant with Down syndrome developing a vision problem are greater. An early eye examination is recommended, with annual visits to an eye doctor thereafter. Proper treatment often prevents the problem from interfering with the child's development or leading to a more serious problem.

The most common eye problem is eye muscle imbalance, a condition known as *strabismus*. Strabismus is a condition in which the eyes cross because of an eye muscle imbalance. This condition occurs in nearly 60 percent of babies born with Down syndrome. The eyes are crossed when one eye muscle is "stronger" than another, pulling the eye in one direction. The other eye may be pulled in an opposite direction, resulting in crossed eyes. Crossed eyes cause decreased vision.

A young child with Down syndrome may need glasses to help correct poor vision.

When the muscle imbalance affects only one eye, the condition is commonly referred to as "lazy eye." In the case of a "lazy eye," the brain may ignore signals it receives from that eye. If the brain continues to ignore these signals, then the eye will fail to develop normally. The eye may even become completely blind. To prevent this from happening, an early examination is extremely important. Because a child's eyes are not fully developed at birth, visual problems are difficult to detect at an early age. For this reason, an eye examination of an infant with Down syndrome should be done by a pediatric ophthalmologist—a doctor who specializes in children's eyes and eye diseases.

Another problem that may develop with the eyes is poor vision. One type of poor vision common in babies with

Down syndrome is nearsightedness. With nearsightedness, objects in the distance are difficult to see. Children with nearsightedness tend to hold books, toys, and other objects close to their eyes. A baby with Down syndrome may be born with the opposite condition, which is known as farsightedness. In this case, objects that are nearby are difficult to see. A child with farsightedness may show no interest in reading or playing board games. Both nearsightedness and farsightedness are easily corrected with eyeglasses or contact lenses.

Another vision problem is *astigmatism,* which occurs in about 20 percent of the infants with Down syndrome. In astigmatism, the eye has an irregular shape. This irregular shape prevents light rays from focusing at a single point on the back of the eye as they do in normal eyes. The images that are formed are blurred. Astigmatism can be detected by an eye examination and treated with eyeglasses or contact lenses.

Two other vision problems that are slightly more common in children with Down syndrome are cataracts and blocked tear ducts. Cataracts form when the lens—the opening in the eye that lets light enter—becomes cloudy. As the cloudiness increases, the vision decreases. Today, surgeons can replace the damaged lens with a new one. Like a blocked eustachian tube, a blocked tear duct can become a site of infection. A blocked tear duct can also interfere with vision. Massaging the eye, along with eye drops, will often unclog the tear duct. In more serious cases, surgery may be necessary.

Weight Problems

Babies with Down syndrome are usually of average weight at birth but shortly after birth, they tend not to gain weight.

As a result, their growth is slower than that of other children. The reduced weight and slower growth are frequently caused by genes the child has inherited. However, feeding problems may contribute to the problem. For example, the low muscle tone makes it difficult for the infant to suck milk and to swallow. Later in life, low muscle tone will occasionally affect the muscles in the jaw, and chewing solid food could become a problem. Without sufficient nourishment, the baby will not gain weight. Special attention to the eating habits of a baby with Down syndrome is very important for normal growth.

Low Muscle Tone

In addition to eating, other activities are also affected by the low muscle tone in babies with Down syndrome. Although the degree of low muscle tone varies from infant to infant, it generally affects every muscle in the body. As a result, the baby moves less. The baby's posture may also be unusual. For example, when lying on its back, the baby's legs may be turned out and spread wide apart. A baby with Down syndrome may also fall asleep with its head in its lap.

These unusual postures are possible because the baby's joints are so flexible. Joints allow bones to move, but only to a certain degree. The greater flexibility of the joints in a baby with Down syndrome is related to low muscle tone. Low muscle tone also affects the development of motor skills. Motor skills depend on the action of muscles. Such skills include crawling, sitting, and walking.

Mental Retardation

Mental retardation that results from Down syndrome can range from mild to severe. Most babies with Down syndrome function in the mild to moderate range of mental retardation. As a result, learning is slower. But a baby with Down syndrome can learn—it just takes a little longer.

Babies with Down syndrome may have a shorter attention span and less motivation than other babies, so new skills have to be practiced in shorter, more frequent lesson periods. For example, the child may have to work with one piece of a puzzle at a time rather than assembling all the pieces at once. Physically touching an object can also help a child with Down syndrome learn concepts. For example, learning to count is easier by having the child touch familiar objects such as cookies or toys rather than just look at pictures of these objects.

Because of their mental retardation, babies with Down syndrome do not develop their intellectual skills as quickly as other children. Normally, a baby between the ages of 12 and 14 months will be able to find a familiar object, such as a favorite toy, that has been hidden from view. Between 12 and 14 months, a baby usually develops the mental skills to put objects in containers. A baby with Down syndrome will be able to accomplish both of these tasks, but at a point later in life. That age depends on the degree of mental retardation.

Overcoming the Problems of Infancy

The problems an infant with Down syndrome faces may seem overwhelming to you. There is no doubt that these problems can be serious and may require advanced medical care and constant parental attention. But in spite of the problems that may arise, an infant with Down syndrome will grow and learn. For example, consider how Jamie Berube, with his family's help, overcame a number of problems as an infant. The story of Jamie is told in a book, *Life As We Know It,* written by his father.

Shortly after birth, Jamie was transferred from the nursery to the intensive care unit. Doctors had detected a number of medical problems, including one involving his circulatory system—a hole failed to close in the heart, allowing blood on both sides to mix. In Jamie's case, the opening was actually between two blood vessels that lead blood away from the heart. Like the channel in the septum of the heart, this opening is normally present in a fetus to allow more blood to flow to the umbilical cord. On the first day of life, the opening between the two blood vessels usually closes. If it does not close, this opening creates the same problem as if it were in the heart—Jamie's blood was not getting enough oxygen.

In addition, Jamie had a problem with his larynx, or voice box. Because of this problem, Jamie could not swallow and breathe normally. Gradually, however, his medical problems began to disappear, one at a time. First, the hole between the two blood vessels closed by itself. As a result, the oxygen level in his blood rose and remained normal. The problem with his larynx also cleared up by itself. After 19 days in the intensive care unit, Jamie was released from the hospital. But going home did not mean that Jamie's problems were over.

At home, he had to be hooked up to a machine that monitored the oxygen level in his blood. This allowed the doctors and his parents to be sure that his heart problem did not reappear. The machine would also warn his parents if he developed sleep apnea. It would give off a piercing sound if anything went wrong with his breathing. Jamie also had to be fed milk through a tube that was lubricated and inserted into his nose, down his pharynx, and into his tiny stomach. Gradually, Jamie was able to drink from a bottle.

Besides sleep apnea, another respiratory problem Jamie had was a narrow trachea. The slightest infection could block this air passageway. To prevent an infection from developing, Jamie's parents washed their hands dozens of times a day and wore surgical face masks whenever they thought they might be developing a cold. They also made visitors go through the same procedures, but their precautions did not always work. Jamie developed one upper respiratory infection after another. Antibiotics were the only solution.

Another medical problem was caused by the abnormally tight muscles in the back of Jamie's neck. These muscles pulled his head to one side so that he could not sit upright. Doctors had recommended a surgical procedure to cut and resew the neck muscles. But Jamie's parents decided against this procedure. Instead, they relied on physical therapy. At first, they took Jamie to a therapist who massaged the muscles in Jamie's neck for an hour at a time. Jamie's parents worked with the therapist to learn how to massage the muscles. When he was six months old, Jamie's neck muscles were finally loose enough to allow him to sit upright.

Tests revealed that Jamie also had moderate to severe hearing loss. Doctors were not sure if the hearing loss was due to a problem with his ears or with his brain. If Jamie's brain were the cause, the problem might not be correctable. Fortunately, the problem was with Jamie's ears—

or one ear, to be precise. The other ear was borderline normal. Speech therapists helped Jamie overcome his hearing problem so that he could develop his language skills.

Jamie's parents monitored his growth as an infant and could not help but compare his development with that of his older brother, Nick, who did not have Down syndrome. At 10 months of age, Nick could point to an object after he had been told its name. He could also recognize relationships among different objects. Jamie was almost twice that age before he could accomplish these same tasks. When he was just over a year old, Nick could point to a letter of the alphabet and say what letter it was. Jamie was 3 years old before he could do that.

With his parents constant care, Jamie eventually managed to overcome the many problems he faced as an infant with Down syndrome. True, he took longer to accomplish what his older brother was able to do, but Jamie eventually accomplished many of the same tasks as other infants. When he was three, Jamie got his first Individualized Education Plan (IEP). With the problems of his infancy behind him, Jamie was now ready to face the challenges of the early school years.

CHAPTER 5

Early School Years

M<small>EDICAL PROBLEMS</small> continue to appear as an infant with Down syndrome gets older and begins schooling. In addition, the child is now out of the home and away from the family for long stretches of time. While growing up at home, the child most likely had siblings who did not have Down syndrome. In school, the child will probably find a "whole world" of normal children. This will certainly be the case if the child is "mainstreamed," which means being placed in regular classes for part of the school day. As a result, the child will now have to develop the social skills needed to gain acceptance from the other children.

This young girl with Down syndrome (second from the left) has been mainstreamed into an after-school ballet class.

Inclusion

Like any other child, a child with Down syndrome wants to be included in all the activities that take place in a normal classroom. In special education, this process is called "inclusion." Inclusion simply means being part of what is going on around you. But being placed in a normal classroom can be a traumatic experience for a child with Down syndrome. Both the teacher and the other students must be sensitive to the child's needs, and they must make every reasonable effort to include the child in classroom activities whenever possible.

Inclusion may mean that a child with Down syndrome is placed in a class where the children are at a similar developmental level. For example, the children may be learning a specific skill that involves working with numbers. An average child may be able to master this particular skill between the ages of 6 and 7, but a child with Down syndrome will probably take longer to acquire the same skill. How much longer depends on the degree of mental retardation. Assume that a child with Down syndrome takes another two years to acquire the same math skill. So it is possible that inclusion results in a nine-year-old child with Down syndrome being placed in a class with children who are two or three years younger. Despite their age differences, all the children will be sharing a similar experience. Moreover they will also be challenged to the same level of their developmental ability.

Inclusion can present problems, however. If the child becomes frustrated, learning will not take place. The child may also become quiet and withdrawn. If inclusion does not seem to be working, the child may learn better in a smaller, more focused classroom. Inclusion can also present a challenge for the teacher who will need to rely upon certain strategies to a greater extent. These strategies are not unique to the education of a child with Down syndrome— they are used with all children in the early school years. In fact, some of these strategies are used at every grade level. But a teacher who is working with a child with Down syndrome will need to use them more often than usual.

Teaching Strategies

Every child in unique, so no single teaching strategy will work for all children. The same, of course, is true for children with Down syndrome. In their case, the IEP developed for each child with Down syndrome will provide the teacher with guidelines and suggestions for working with that particular child. Among the IEPs for children with Down syndrome, teachers will most likely find the following suggested strategies.

Divide every learning task into small steps. In learning to assemble a simple puzzle, an infant with Down syndrome may have to put the same piece in its correct spot a number of times before attempting to place the next piece. Consider how a child with Down syndrome might learn how to identify an object that does not belong in the same group as the others. For example, one object may be rectangular while all the others have a round shape. Rather than place all the objects together and look for the one that is different, the teacher may take one object with a round shape and compare it to the others one at a time.

A learning task may have to be repeated. In the example above, the teacher may have to repeat the procedure a number of times, selecting a different round object each time to compare with the others. After doing this a number of times, the teacher may then ask the child to identify the one that does not belong from among all the objects that have been placed together.

Patience and persistence are required. Children with Down syndrome are apt to have a shorter attention span, so they may quickly lose interest in what the teacher is trying to do. Similarly, the teacher may find the lesson boring, especially if the task has to be repeated a number of times. Rather than give up, the teacher can reduce the number of objects that were originally used. The time spent on each task then becomes shorter, resulting in less of a challenge to the attention span of the child and the patience of the teacher.

Expectations must be well defined. The teacher must know exactly what learning task the child is expected to accomplish successfully. Obviously, the teacher is not expecting the child to identify the one object that differs only among those that have been chosen for that particular lesson. Rather the expectation is that the child will learn to recognize similarities and differences in any given situation. So this specific learning task is really a step to a much broader expectation. When this specific task has been accomplished, then the child is ready for the next step on the way to meeting this expectation. With the expectation clearly in mind, the teacher will then select a completely different group of objects for the child to investigate.

Consistency and a positive approach are critical. Not having a consistent pattern and routine can be very upsetting to a child. In addition, a child must be given praise or some other reward when a task is successfully accomplished. Children with Down syndrome are no different. The teacher must be sure to say "no" when the child selects the incorrect object and be sure to reward the child when the correct object is chosen. The reward may be as simple as allowing the child to play with a favorite toy or listen to a favorite song.

Possible Educational Environments

In addition to inclusion and mainstreaming, there are several possible educational environments in which a child with Down syndrome can be placed. Each child with Down syndrome has different educational needs, so an educational environment that is right for one child will not necessarily be appropriate for another. The IEP for each child should help decide which educational environment will be best for that child. In addition, the educational needs of any child—especially one with Down syndrome—change over time. As a child with Down syndrome progresses through the early school years, the child may move from one environment to another. There are five possible environments in which the child may be educated in a public school.

1) Regular classroom

This environment would be a self-contained classroom where one teacher is solely responsible for educating the children. This kind of classroom is suitable for only a small number of children with Down syndrome because a number of conditions must be satisfied. The child must not have a serious medical problem and must have an IQ near the normal range. The child must also fit in socially with the other children. Most classroom teachers have not been trained to deal with students with special needs, so the class size should be small. Then the teacher has the opportunity and time to use the teaching strategies described earlier. However, if the child with Down syndrome fails to learn in such an environment, placement in a different setting should be considered immediately. Otherwise, the child's self-image may be negatively affected.

2) Regular classroom with additional services

As a result of the laws that you read about in Chapter 2, educators who are trained to deal with learning disabled children must be available in all public schools. The educator might be a special education teacher who meets with the regular classroom teacher to discuss the best ways to help the child with Down syndrome. Even in this educa-

A child with Down syndrome can feel comfortable and confident spending part of the school day in a "normal" class.

tional environment, the child must be able to function very close to the average level, both intellectually and physically.

Some schools may provide a part-time special education teacher to work with a child with Down syndrome. This teacher can work with the child on a one-to-one basis, reinforcing what has been taught by the regular classroom teacher. The part-time teacher can also focus on social skills by working with a group that includes the child with Down syndrome and several classmates. In the meantime, the regular classroom teacher would be working with the other children.

3) Regular classroom with time in a resource room

In this environment, the child with Down syndrome would spend part of each day with a special education teacher in a resource room. The child would spend the rest of the day in a regular classroom. This environment provides the extra instruction and support the child needs, while allowing the child to be part of an ordinary class the rest of the time. This environment can work well for Down syndrome children who have a mild degree of mental retardation.

4) Resource room with time in a regular classroom

This environment is similar to the one previously described, except the time spent in each room is reversed. Most of the school day is spent in a resource room where the child learns academic skills. Time spent in the regular classroom would focus on physical and social skills. This environment is best suited for Down syndrome children who have a moderate degree of mental retardation.

5) Resource room

For Down syndrome children with severe mental retardation or multiple physical disabilities, the resource room may be the best educational environment. Here the child can receive all the attention and care that are needed. Contact with the other children in school can still occur during lunch, recess, and dismissal times.

Some children with Down syndrome will not be able to function in any of these school settings. Their mental condition may require that they receive a very structured and restricted environment. In addition, the school may not be equipped to handle the type of emergency that can arise from a medical problem the child has. In such cases, the parents have two options. They can send their child to a full-time special school, where there is close supervision and numerous support services for learning disabled children. Or, they can send their child to a residential special school. This type of educational environment is similar to a boarding school. In a residential special school, the child may spend the week at school and return home for the weekends. Such schools are best suited for children with Down syndrome who have severe physical disabilities and are creating serious behavior problems at home.

Medical Problems

No matter what educational environment a child with Down syndrome experiences, involvement in gym activities often needs to be adapted to some extent. Physical features such as low muscle tone, and medical problems such as limited hearing may restrict the child's physical activity in school. Another medical problem that can also affect a child's stamina involves the thyroid gland.

The *thyroid gland* is a tiny gland located near the trachea in the neck. The thyroid gland produces a *hormone*—a chemical substance that is produced in one part of the body but acts in another part of the body. The hormone that the thyroid gland produces is called *thyroxin*. Thyroxin is secreted into the bloodstream and then travels throughout the body. Thyroxin promotes the normal growth of the brain, bones, and muscles during childhood.

Thyroxin also regulates the rate of many body functions. These functions include how well the body uses sugar and oxygen for energy. In effect, thyroxin helps control *metabolism,* which represents all the processes that occur in the body. Metabolism provides the body with energy. The more thyroxin produced, the higher the metabolism, and the higher the energy level. On the other hand, the less thyroxin produced, the lower the metabolism, and the lower the energy level.

In children with Down syndrome, the thyroid gland tends to be less active. This condition is known as *hypothyroidism.* Approximately 10 percent of children with Down syndrome have hypothyroidism. In hypothyroidism, the thyroid gland actually becomes larger. The gland gets larger because it is trying to make more thyroxin, but without any success. The more it tries, the larger it gets. Eventually, the enlarged gland can become very noticeable.

Besides the larger size of the thyroid gland, symptoms of hypothyroidism include a decreased energy level, delayed physical and mental development, and sleepiness. This condition can also be recognized in early school-age children by looking for muscle cramps and a dry, thickened skin. The child may also feel cold all the time. If left untreated, hypothyroidism can result in permanent brain damage, so an immediate blood test is performed if any of these symptoms appear. This test measures the level of thyroxin circulating in the blood. If the level is too low, a pill containing the hormone is prescribed to correct the problem. Usually, only one pill a day is needed. However, the pill will likely have to be taken for the rest of the child's life.

Problems with Bones

Other medical problems that can arise involve the bones. Disorders involving bones are known as *orthopedic* problems. These orthopedic problems develop because of low muscle tone and increased flexibility of the joints. Orthopedic problems usually do not affect a baby with Down syndrome but they begin to appear as the child reaches school age.

The most serious problem affects the two upper verte-brae. The *vertebrae* are the bones that make up the spinal cord, or the backbone. Because of low muscle tone and increased joint flexibility, these two upper vertebrae have greater freedom of movement. This condition appears in about 10 percent of children with Down syndrome. Children who have this condition run a greater risk of spinal cord injury because the two upper vertebrae allow the spinal cord to bend too much. This bending may result in damage to the nerves that run through the spinal cord. Obviously, such children may not participate in any contact sports in school. They also may not do somersaults, tram-poline exercises, or any other gymnastic activity that may cause excess stress on their necks.

About 1 to 2 percent of children with this condition develop a more serious problem. In their case, the two upper vertebrae may actually move apart from each anoth-er. When this happens, the two vertebrae put pressure on the nerves that travel through the spinal cord. This can lead to neck pain, difficulty in walking, and constant con-traction of the neck muscles. To keep the vertebrae from moving apart, children with this condition routinely receive X rays of the neck starting at about five years of age. If a problem is detected, an orthopedic doctor is contacted. Surgery may be necessary to fuse the two vertebrae togeth-er so that they cannot move independently of each anoth-er. This surgery does not affect the child's normal move-ments or growth pattern.

Two other orthopedic problems that can appear in chil-dren with Down syndrome include flat feet and an abnor-mal toeing-in of the foot. These problems result from loose joints that prevent a support arch from forming and cause flat feet, or prevent the feet from pointing straight ahead, and cause toeing-in. Both conditions can be painful and cause difficulty in walking. These problems can be treated with special shoes or corrective supports worn inside the shoes. In more serious cases, surgery may be required. In addition to the feet, the kneecaps may also be affected. The loose joints may allow the kneecap to "pop" out of place, causing swelling and pain. This problem can be corrected with surgery.

Because of the various orthopedic problems that can arise, the American Academy of Pediatrics has issued a set of recommendations for children with Down syndrome who are beginning school. One recommendation is that all children with Down syndrome who wish to participate in a contact sport in gym have X rays to determine the condition of their upper two vertebrae. Children with any signs of vertebrae problems should be restricted from strenuous activities. Children with no signs of a problem should be allowed to participate in all gym activities.

Dental Problems

Although a child with Down syndrome may have healthy teeth and gums as a preschooler, problems tend to arise during the early school years. The teeth may become crowded, crooked, or out of alignment. These problems are likely to start developing when the child reaches the age of six and the "baby" or primary teeth start to be replaced by permanent teeth. With a smaller head size, a child with Down syndrome is likely to have a smaller jaw. The teeth, however, may be normal size. As a result, the teeth can easily become crowded or crooked as they replace the smaller primary teeth.

Teeth that are crooked or crowded can lead to various problems. Such teeth are more difficult to clean because some of their surfaces are difficult to reach. Over time, tooth decay can start and cavities can form. Irregular teeth can also cause chewing problems. The child may favor foods that are easier to chew, refusing many that are essential for good nutrition. Thus crooked and crowded teeth may lead to a poor diet.

The gums may also be affected. Children with Down syndrome are more likely to have soft gums, which in turn can lead to gum diseases. Soft gums may also result in a lost tooth. Playing a contact sport or being actively involved in some activity in school increases the chances of getting a mouth injury. A blow to the mouth may knock a tooth loose.

Proper dental hygiene is important for everyone, but especially for children with Down syndrome. This includes regular brushing, flossing, a nutritious diet, and regular visits to the dentist. Not only will proper dental hygiene reduce the chances of developing a dental problem, but it will help avoid a possible social problem. A child with Down syndrome has distinct facial features, and irregular teeth can affect the child's appearance even more. Other children may be more likely to make comments that upset the child. Social concerns become even more important as the child becomes an adolescent.

CHAPTER 6

Adolescence

ADOLESCENCE is a huge transition period in life. At the onset of adolescence, a child begins to undergo the early stages of reproductive maturity. By the end of adolescence, the child will be reproductively mature. Reproductive maturity is also known as *puberty*. Adolescence can start as early as age 8 and is usually completed by age 16. During this time, a number of behavioral and physical changes occur. Children with Down syndrome experience the same sequence of changes as they progress through adolescence.

Sex Hormones

The changes that occur during adolescence are brought about by hormones. These hormones are essential in the development of sexual maturity and are appropriately

65

A teen with Down syndrome enjoys time with friends.

referred to as the *sex hormones*. The level of sex hormones actually begins to increase in both males and females before any physical changes become noticeable. Some two years before any signs of a physical change, a small gland at the base of the brain starts to produce various hormones. This gland is the *pituitary gland,* which is often called the master gland because it controls a number of other glands.

In males, hormones from the pituitary gland stimulate the *testes,* the male sex organs. In response, the testes start to produce *testosterone,* the male sex hormone. As the testosterone level rises, certain physical changes become apparent. The first visible change is an enlargement in the size of the testes. Hair starts to appear on the face, in the armpits, and in the pubic area. Increasing testosterone levels also cause a male's voice to deepen and his body to get taller. This growth in height may occur in spurts. The sexual maturation process is complete when the male is able to produce mature sperm that can participate in fertilization.

In females, hormones from the pituitary stimulate the *ovaries,* the female sex organs. In response, the ovaries start to produce *estrogen,* the female sex hormone. As the estrogen level rises, certain physical changes become apparent. The first visible change is an enlargement in the size of the breasts. One breast may enlarge more quickly than the other, but eventually both will be about the same size. Hair will appear in the armpit and pubic areas. Like males, females will also experience spurts in their growth. The sexual maturation process is complete when *menstruation* begins. Menstruation is a 28-day cycle in which a female produces an egg cell in preparation for possible fertilization. Commonly referred to as a "period," menstruation involves a number of hormones whose levels change during the 28-day cycle.

Obviously, adolescence is marked by drastic changes in hormone levels. In females especially, hormone levels shift dramatically within the 28-day cycle of menstruation. Along with these changes in hormone levels, a number of other changes also take place. Some of these involve temporary changes in behavior.

Changes in Behavior

Perhaps the most noticeable change in behavior will be "mood swings." One moment, the child may be quiet and withdrawn and just a short time later, the child may be loud and hyperactive. All adolescents experience these sudden "swings" in behavior because of the hormone changes taking place in their bodies, but they can be even more pronounced in adolescents with Down syndrome.

Children with Down Syndrome tire more easily because of their low muscle tone, and growth spurts during adolescence can increase this fatigue. At times, the child may be extremely quiet and withdrawn. As adolescence progresses, the child may have to get more sleep at night and take naps whenever possible.

At other times, the child will respond in just the opposite way. As hormone levels change, the child may become hyperactive and even irritable. A drastic change in hormone levels may even cause the child to display an outburst of anger—a "temper tantrum." Teachers will have to be aware of anything in the educational environment that might bring on such an outburst—music that may be too loud or other children who might be fidgeting. At times, the teacher and other students in the class will have to be extremely patient as a child with Down syndrome passes through adolescence.

Eating behaviors may also change during adolescence. An infant with Down syndrome may not gain weight as quickly as other children. After infancy, however, the situation often changes. Approximately 30 percent of adolescents with Down syndrome develop obesity. This sudden change is due to several factors. Because of their low muscle tone, such children are less active. They may also be inactive because of a possible thyroid problem or heart defect. Increases in hormone levels cause an increased appetite. And of course, eating more and exercising less are the perfect combination for gaining weight.

Many adolescents with Down syndrome will have to be careful about what they eat. But it usually is not necessary to restrict calories so that weight is lost. The child is growing rapidly so, as long as no additional pounds are added, the weight will be redistributed as the child gets taller. If the

Team sports help children with Down syndrome develop
coordination and a sense of belonging.

child is truly obese, however, then dieting to lose weight will be necessary. In such cases, a professional dietitian can be consulted. A dietitian can establish a diet for an overweight adolescent with Down syndrome.

A regular exercise program is also a good way to lose weight. For an adolescent with Down syndrome, the exercise should be enjoyable and free of risk. Because some children with Down syndrome have a problem with their upper two vertebrae, any exercise program that involves stress on the back, such as weight lifting and push-ups, is not appropriate. Swimming is often a good exercise for adolescents with Down syndrome. When swimming is not possible, a planned program of aerobic exercise is another effective and safe way to lose weight.

Special care must be taken if a child with Down syndrome undertakes a regular exercise program. All adolescents tend to be clumsy and somewhat uncoordinated in their movements. Because some parts of the body grow faster than others, the body is out of proportion and the adolescent at times is unable to move in a coordinated fashion. By the end of adolescence, body parts will be back in their normal proportion. In the meantime, parents and teachers of an adolescent with Down syndrome must be reasonable in their expectations of what the child can do physically.

Personal Hygiene

The hormone changes that occur during adolescence also affect the sweat glands. Perspiration begins to have a stronger odor. Most children will notice the odor and begin to wash with soap more thoroughly, especially under their arms. They will also begin to use a deodorant. But adolescents with Down syndrome need to be shown how to wash carefully and told to use a deodorant. Because of their dry skin, younger children with Down syndrome may not use soap to wash. But, during adolescence, soap becomes a necessity. To prevent further drying of the skin, a soap that contains a moisturizing cream can be used.

Learning Everyday Skills

Normally, adolescents learn many everyday skills simply by watching others. For example, a young man may learn how to shave by watching his father, and a young woman may learn how to apply makeup by observing her mother. On the other hand, adolescents with Down syndrome need to be taught many everyday skills. For that reason, adolescents with Down syndrome are much more dependent on older people, especially their parents.

Like any parent, parents of a child with Down syndrome are naturally protective. However, they know that their child is more vulnerable than most other children. A child with Down syndrome can have a number of medical problems. In addition, that child may be the target of negative comments from peers. So, parents of a child with Down syndrome, like those of any child with a disability, will be even more protective than other parents.

Adolescence is often the time when parents begin to allow their child more independence. But for the parents of an adolescent with Down syndrome, this can be a difficult decision to make. Once the decision is made, the process of becoming independent will be very slow for an adolescent with Down syndrome. Like any task, learning how to become independent must done in a series of steps, and each step may have to be repeated a number of times. This is especially true when it comes to learning about their own sexuality.

Learning About Sexuality

Teaching their children about sexuality is often not an easy task for parents. In fact, some parents may leave the issue of sex education entirely up to the school. Most schools include sex education as part of their health curriculum in the sixth grade, but a child with Down syndrome may not be included in this program. In that case, the parents have total responsibility for teaching their child about sexuality.

When to start teaching a child about sexuality is just as important as who will teach them. There is no one point in life that is best. However, a good time to start dealing with the child's sex education is at the start of adolescence, perhaps as early as age eight. Children should be prepared for the physical changes that will occur in their bodies. Not knowing why certain things are happening can be frightening for any child, especially one with Down syndrome. The best place to start is probably a description of the physical changes the child will experience. For example, boys should be told about the hair that will develop and that their voices will deepen. Girls should be told that their breasts will get larger and that their menstrual cycles will start.

Menstruation is difficult for any girl to understand at first, and it is even more so for a girl with Down syndrome. Most adolescent girls with Down syndrome, however, manage their menstruation well. Parents need to emphasize that the girl has taken the first step to becoming a mature woman, and a gift to mark the occasion can help the girl through this difficult transition. Parents do not need to go through all the details of menstruation that a teacher may cover in a health class. They should simply explain what menstruation means and provide practical advice on how to deal with it. The girl will also have to be told that menstruation is not something that is discussed freely with just anyone.

Now that they are reproductively mature, adolescents with Down syndrome must also be informed about the danger of sexual abuse. Unfortunately, individuals with mental retardation are often more vulnerable to sexual abuse than others. Parents must be sure that their child learns how to ward off sexual harassment or abuse. Adolescents with Down syndrome, however, may not be able to learn how to protect themselves in various situations. For example, they may not be able to distinguish between acceptable and unacceptable ways for a family member to touch them.

One way to teach adolescents with Down syndrome how to prevent sexual abuse involves creating "circles of social distance" that can be drawn up by a parent or teacher. Each circle is shaded a different color. The child is told that the innermost circle is the "self circle." Moving outward, the remaining circles are "family circle," "friend circle," "acquaintance circle," and "stranger circle." Each circle represents a different degree of social acceptance. Each circle can be referred to by its color to make it easier for the child to remember what it represents.

The "self circle" represents the child, who can touch his or her own body freely. The "family circle" represents close relatives, who can be hugged and kissed. Those in the "friend circle" can be waved to and hugged. People in the "acquaintance circle" can be greeted with a handshake. Finally, anyone in the "stranger circle" should not be touched in any way. People with whom the child comes in contact should then be placed in the appropriate circle. A teacher, for example, falls in the "acquaintance circle." Thus the child can say goodbye to a teacher by shaking hands, but not with a hug. Hugs are reserved for anyone in the "friend circle" or a sibling in the "family circle."

Learning About Responsibilities

Adolescents need to socialize with one another, especially those of the opposite sex. This is even more important for adolescents with Down syndrome. Only through social contacts will an adolescent learn proper social behaviors, accept responsibilities, and develop a sense of independence. Many social behaviors and responsibilities seem obvious to the average adolescent. For example, most adolescents realize that interrupting a conversation is not an acceptable behavior and that cleaning up after dinner is everyone's responsibility. But an adolescent with Down syndrome has to be told exactly what is acceptable and expected, and exactly what is not. Repetition will be necessary before the proper behavior is learned and responsibility is assumed.

Sending the adolescent on a specific errand can also help promote such learning. Like any other learning task, the errand must be broken down into several small steps. For example, parents may want their son or daughter to be able to walk to the local grocery store to buy a container of milk. First the child will have to be shown how to get to the store. Crossing streets safely, especially streets without traffic lights, requires the ability to make judgments. This step alone may take considerable time to learn. Next, the child will have to be shown where the dairy section is located in the store. Then the child will need to be taken to the checkout counter and shown how to pay for the milk. Finally, the child must be shown how to return home.

At first, a parent will have to accompany the child a number of times as they complete the errand. Gradually, the parent can begin to cut down on the help provided. For example, the parent may assist until the milk is picked up but then allow the child to bring it to the counter and pay for it. Once this step has been mastered, the parent may allow the child to enter the store alone. Eventually, the child will be able to perform the entire task alone.

Before performing the task alone, however, the child will have to learn how to deal with money. Again, what seems like common sense to most adolescents will take time for someone with Down syndrome to learn. The child must be taught how to recognize different denominations of money and how to make change. As part of the IEP in school, the child may be studying math concepts that will help in learning how to count money.

Shopping for a grocery product is just one independent living skill. An adolescent with Down syndrome will also need to learn how to prepare meals, wash clothes, keep a clean house, use public transportation, go to the movies, and do any other activity that is part of a person's normal routine. Only then will the adolescent be prepared for adulthood and the time when he or she may move away from home. But before they do, there is one more thing they learn as adolescents. They begin to be aware of their disability.

Learning About One's Own Disability

All children start to compare themselves to others at an early age. But during adolescence children with Down syndrome begin to ask their parents why they are different from other children. Parents must discuss the condition with their child as soon as the child is able to understand. Hearing about their condition first from their parents can prevent a lot of grief. Unfortunately, too many children with Down syndrome first learn of their condition from other children. In many cases, what they hear is derogatory and painful.

Adolescents with Down syndrome often assume that they are related to others with the same condition because they look alike in some ways. Parents need to point out that each child has a family of his or her own. In fact, a child with Down syndrome looks more like his or her own parents than like other children with Down syndrome. Whenever possible, parents should point out the features that members of their family share. For example, a child with Down syndrome may have the same eye color as the mother or the same hair color as the father. Parents also need to emphasize that despite the disability, children with Down syndrome are talented in various ways. They can point to something special the child has accomplished. Parents should mention that some things will be more difficult for children with Down syndrome, no matter how hard they try. In this way, they can prevent their child from becoming frustrated. Most importantly, the parents should emphasize that every child is unique, with special abilities and talents. Only by trying will the child be able to know what these abilities and talents are. Consider what Chris Burke was able to accomplish despite having Down syndrome.

A National Spokesperson

Born with Down syndrome, Chris Burke had a lifelong dream to become an actor despite his disability. His hard work and persistent efforts proved to be successful. Chris played a character called Corky for four years on a network television show called "Life Goes On." In addition, he has appeared in various roles in other television shows, including "Touched by An Angel," and was featured on an episode of "48 Hours."

In addition to his acting, Chris also enjoys singing. In 1997, he participated in a conference that featured programs for adolescents and adults with Down syndrome. In one event, Chris teamed up with country singer Buc Williams for a couple of songs. Today, Chris tours the

United States giving talks to children, parents, and medical professionals about what individuals with Down syndrome can accomplish. Each year, he leads the way in the annual "Buddy Walk" in New York City. Held in various cities throughout the country, the "Buddy Walk" is aimed at promoting community awareness about Down syndrome.

Chris Burke (front, kneeling) played Corky on the popular TV series "Life Goes On."

When he isn't busy acting, singing, or speaking, Chris serves as editor-in-chief of his own magazine about Down syndrome, called *News and Views*. The magazine is published four times a year and features stories and information about people like Chris who have succeeded in some way despite having Down syndrome. As part of his role as editor-in-chief, Chris also interviews entertainment stars and responds to readers' questions. In 1997, Chris found the time to serve as the National Down Syndrome Society's Goodwill Ambassador, making public appearances on their behalf to promote the services provided by this organization.

Adulthood

IN THE EARLY 1900s children with Down syndrome were not expected to live much past the age of nine. Mainly because of advances in medicine, people with Down syndrome are living much longer today. This longer life span means that parents must prepare for the time when their child with Down syndrome reaches adulthood. At this stage in life, people with Down syndrome must make some decisions that will affect the rest of their lives. Perhaps the most important decision will be where they will live as adults. In the past, it was common for adults with Down syndrome to remain with their parents. Today, an increasing number of adults with Down syndrome live away from home and assume most of the responsibilities for their daily needs.

A young woman with Down syndrome attends a wedding with her family.

The time comes when the family of a child with Down syndrome must discuss future living arrangements. This is often an extremely difficult period for those concerned—almost everyone has mixed feelings. Parents are naturally concerned about whether their child can function independently. These parents must realize that the goal of parenthood is to prepare a child to live as independently as possible upon becoming an adult.

Parents will also have to realize that living at home might solve some short-term problems, but a much more serious problem may arise at some point in the future. If adults with Down syndrome remain at home, they may continue to rely on their parents for their daily needs. When the parents become too old or ill, they will no longer be able to provide much care or support. Suddenly, an adult with Down syndrome may have to cope without his or her parents, and this may prove too much to handle. In addition to what might happen in the future, there are other factors to consider when an adult with Down syndrome starts to think about moving out of the home.

Factors to Consider

A major factor to consider is how well the adult can function on his or her own. Much will depend on what the parents did to help the individual become independent during adolescence. No matter how independent they have become, adults with Down syndrome will always need more help than the average person. Of course, the amount of help needed will vary. Most will need some help in dealing with financial matters. Someone will need to check that their bills are being paid and that money is available for emergencies. Most adults with Down syndrome will also need help in dealing with such matters as preparing tax returns and completing health insurance forms. Those adults who need help in taking care of their basic needs will probably never be able to leave home. But most adults with Down syndrome are able to take some responsibility for their daily needs, such as shopping for food and clothes, preparing meals, doing household chores, and perhaps even meeting the requirements of a job. At times, they may need help from another adult.

The degree to which the adult can function independently is only one factor to consider when deciding whether to leave the home. An adult with Down syndrome must also be able, both physically and emotionally, to get out and socialize. Even if the adult can take care of all the necessary basic needs, living on one's own would not be a good idea if the person simply stays at home alone all the time. Such an adult can easily become depressed.

Moving out of the home can also relieve stress among family members. Taking care of someone with Down syndrome from infancy to adulthood can place a great deal of stress on the entire family. Moving out of the home will relieve this stress and enable the family to function like most other families. If there are other children in the family, parents will be able to spend more time with them. These children, by necessity, could not receive as much attention while growing up as did their sibling with Down syndrome.

At one time, the intellectual ability of the person was a major factor in deciding whether an adult with Down syndrome could live away from home. As you know, most persons with Down syndrome have some degree of mental retardation. Like any other person with mental retardation, an adult with Down syndrome can be said to have two ages. One is their actual age in years; the other is their intellectual age as reflected in their IQ or ability to perform some mental task. In the past, parents were often told to treat their child with Down syndrome according to his or her intellectual age. As a result, adults with Down syndrome were often treated as children. Parents dressed them, spoke to them, and entertained them as if they were children.

In the early 1960s, opposition to this kind of treatment was raised. Today, professionals realize that the IQ of a person with Down syndrome does not necessarily reflect his or her ability to function in society. For example, an individual with Down syndrome may understand the meaning of each word but have difficulty putting them together in a sentence with the correct grammar. Parents are now told to consider their son or daughter with Down syndrome according to his or her actual age. Thus an adult with Down syndrome should be dressed like any other adult and taken to the same kinds of places. Federal laws have made it possible for adults with Down syndrome to use public places and facilities.

Where to Live

The early 1960s also marked another milestone in the story of Down syndrome. At that time, parents of children with Down syndrome began insisting that their sons and daughters should have the same rights and opportunities as other adults. Their stance led to the closing of many institutions where adults with Down syndrome had been placed. Today, an adult with Down syndrome has several options about where to live. The choice depends on what is available in the local community, and on the needs and skills of the adult.

One choice is a residence. A residence actually consists of several buildings clustered together. Each building is self-contained with its own sleeping, dining, and social areas. In addition, each building contains classrooms and meeting rooms where parents may visit their son or daughter. The residents are housed in a building on the basis of sex, age, and degree of independence. In some cases, however, age may not be a factor, so a building may house people of all ages, from young adults to senior citizens.

Regardless of their age, all the needs of the people are met within the residence. Everyone who lives in a residence requires assistance with their normal everyday tasks. In addition, they need considerable medical attention. Thus people living in a residence are not likely to be part of their community. They cannot just leave when they wish to walk through the park or visit friends. However, the needs of these people are often better served in a residence than they would be at home.

Daily chores are shared in an adult group home.

Another possibility for an adult with Down syndrome who is moving out is a group home. Group homes are for adults with Down syndrome who can function independently to some degree. As its name suggests, a group home accommodates a group of people—usually between three and six—who have some form of disability. Each state licenses and operates group homes. State regulations determine how many people can live in the group home, what types of disabilities the adults can have, and what ages are permitted. For example, a group home may be licensed to house four adults aged 20 or older who have mild to moderate mental retardation.

Today, many adults with Down syndrome live in group homes. Adults of both sexes often share a group home. Each person has his or her own room furnished with personal possessions. The adults share a common living and eating area as well as the responsibilities of daily living. The adults can leave the home at any time to go to work, visit friends, or see a movie.

In a group home, staff members are on duty 24 hours a day to make sure that all the needs of the residents are met. This may mean no more than dropping by the home to make sure that everything is running smoothly. For example, they may stop by to dispense medications that an adult must take, check that nutritious meals are being prepared, and make sure the house is clean and orderly. The residents of some group homes may be more severely disabled than those in other group homes. In such cases, a staff member may have to live in the home and do the cooking and cleaning. A group home must also provide health and rehabilitation services for each resident. The types of services are agreed upon in writing by both the adult's parents and the group home staff.

In a group home, an adult has the opportunity to interact with other adults as well as members of the community. The adult can take part in any of the activities available to the rest of the community. They may visit friends or walk through the local park. To make a group home seem more homelike, attempts are made to keep the number of residents to less than 10 adults.

For those adults with Down syndrome who are truly independent, another option is available. This is known as a semi-independent living service program. This program is designed for a disabled adult aged 18 or older who can live independently. In this program, two to four people share an apartment or a small house. The residents are responsible for maintaining and running the household. They must pay the bills, buy the food, prepare the meals, and do the cleaning. Each resident must have a source of income and be able to budget his or her money. In effect, the residents assume total responsibility for their daily lives. Support staff is limited to a few evening hours a week. However, a staff member is always available if a resident needs assistance. Because this program is the closest to an average home, it is in great demand.

Some adults with Down syndrome may be able to live completely alone. They may be able to perform all the daily chores, from preparing meals to paying bills. But living alone can lead to total isolation for an adult with Down syndrome who has very limited social contacts. In turn, isolation may lead to depression. Thus, living completely alone is not generally recommended for an adult with Down syndrome.

Getting a Job

Living away from home will probably mean that an adult with Down syndrome will have some financial responsibilities to meet. The more independence the adult has, the greater these responsibilities will be. For example, the adult is likely to have entertainment expenses. These include eating out, going to the movies, and taking short trips. Many of the adults with Down syndrome who decide to leave home seek a job to help pay for these expenses and can become successfully employed. Two basic types of employment are available to adults with Down syndrome.

*Many adults with Down syndrome have the intelligence
and skills to work at a job.*

First, they can join the ranks of those looking for a job in
the regular work world. Adults with Down syndrome have
obtained jobs as cashiers, clerks, messengers, short-order
cooks, warehouse laborers, theater ushers, waiters, and
waitresses. Some companies and businesses even have a policy of employing people with disabilities whenever possible.
Companies and businesses are required by law to follow certain regulations when hiring people with disabilities.

The American with Disabilities Act passed by Congress in
1990 prohibits an employer from discriminating against a
qualified person because of a disability. The law defines a
"qualified individual with a disability" as a person with a disability who can perform the essential functions of a job with
or without reasonable accommodation. "Reasonable ac-

commodation" means that an employer must make an effort to remove any obstacle that would prevent the person from performing the job. The obstacle might be the physical facility where the employees work. For example, if the adult with a disability is confined to a wheelchair, a ramp may have to be installed. Or the obstacle might be the schedule. Travel arrangements may make it impossible for an adult with Down syndrome to arrive at a certain time. If possible, the employer must shuffle the schedule to accommodate the adult's travel arrangements. In all cases, the accommodations must be "reasonable" for the employer who is not required to incur any "undue hardship" by hiring a person with a disability. But failing to make a "reasonable accommodation" places the employer in violation of a federal law.

If an adult with Down syndrome gets a regular job, he or she will need certain qualities to succeed at the job. First, the adult must have near-normal intelligence. In addition, the adult must be able to function independently because a supervisor will not be able to constantly monitor the worker's job performance. The chances of succeeding in the job are also greater if the adult has had experience in a school-to-work program in high school. Such programs teach students the basic responsibilities of having a job, proper dress codes, and appropriate behavior with coworkers.

An adult with Down syndrome may have the necessary intelligence and skills but lack the self-reliance and confidence needed to function in a regular job. The job will probably be stressful at times, causing the adult to become agitated. Working in a regular job also exposes the adult with Down syndrome to possible abuse and exploitation by coworkers and customers. If business becomes slow, the adult may lose his or her job. Rather than recognize the true cause, the adult may feel responsible for losing the job and become depressed. For these reasons, a regular job may not be a good idea for many adults with Down syndrome. In such cases, another job option is available.

An adult with Down syndrome can seek a job in sheltered employment. As its name implies, sheltered employment does not expose the person to the pressure and demands of a regular job. Instead the adult with Down syndrome works along with others who have an intellectual disability. The work is performed in a supervised environment where trained staff members assist anyone needing help. The work is more structured than most jobs. For example, the adult may be part of an assembly process where a piece of equipment is manufactured. Or the adult may be responsible for packaging a consumer product for shipment. Whenever possible, the work performed by each individual is varied to prevent boredom. Breaks during the workday allow for socialization and recreation between employees.

No matter where adults with Down syndrome work, their self-image and sense of independence are enhanced by knowing that they are being productive. They may also have the opportunity to bring their skills and talents to the job. In return, the regular paycheck that they receive will give the adult a sense of satisfaction from a job well done.

Marriage

Moving out of the home and getting a job are not the only major milestones an adult with Down syndrome must face. Getting married is another one. As more adults with

Down syndrome become active members of society, the possibility of marriage becomes more likely. In the past, marriage was not considered an issue for adults with Down syndrome, as these adults seldom got married. If they did, they usually married a person who also had an intellectual disability. Rarely did an adult with Down syndrome marry someone who had no disability.

Most people believed adults with Down syndrome were reproductively immature and thus discouraged them from marrying. But adolescents with Down syndrome reach reproductive maturity just as others their age do. Adults with Down syndrome can marry and have children. They can also be susceptible to sexually transmitted diseases.

Adolescent females with Down syndrome develop a regular menstrual cycle or "period." Scientific studies have shown that at least half of all women with Down syndrome are fertile. This means that during their menstrual cycle, they can produce an egg cell that is capable of being fertilized. A major concern would be the chances of this woman having a child with Down syndrome. The answer depends in part on what caused her to have Down syndrome.

Ninety-five percent of Down syndrome cases are caused by an extra chromosome 21 or trisomy 21. If a fertile female has trisomy 21, there is a chance that an egg cell she produces will contain an extra chromosome 21. To know exactly what that chance is, a diagram or a grid is often used. Such a grid is called a *Punnett square*. A Punnett square is a method used to determine the chance of a particular event occurring as a result of fertilization. For example, a Punnett square can show why there is a 50 percent chance that a

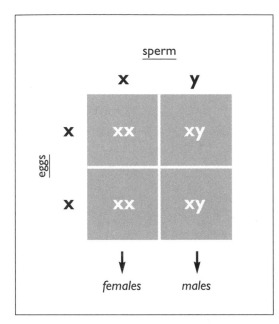

A Punnett square showing how the sex of a child is determined

newborn will be a male, and a 50 percent chance that it will be a female.

A female has an XX chromosome combination, while a male has an XY chromosome combination. As a result of meiosis, each egg cell the woman produces will normally contain one X chromosome. On the other hand, the male will produce sperm cells, half of which contain an X chromosome, the other half a Y chromosome. Upon fertilization, there is a 50 percent chance that the fertilized egg will contain an XX combination and thus be a female. There is also a 50 percent chance that the fertilized egg will contain an XY combination and thus be a male.

Now consider what might happen when a woman with Down syndrome has a child. There is a chance that her egg cell contains an extra chromosome 21. Assume that the male produces normal sperm, each containing only one copy of chromosome 21. If a sperm fertilizes the egg with only one copy of chromosome 21, the result will be a child who does not have Down syndrome. However, if a sperm fertilizes the egg that contains two copies of chromosome 21, then the baby will have trisomy 21 or Down syndrome. So the chances of a woman with Down syndrome having a baby with the same condition is 50 percent, a figure supported by the medical reports. Of the 21 cases reported in medical journals of a mother with Down syndrome giving birth, ten of the babies also had Down syndrome. This represents 48 percent of the babies born to mothers with Down syndrome.

Information in medical journals about fertility in adult males with Down syndrome is limited, but men with Down syndrome seem to be less fertile than other men of the same age. There is only one case on record of a male with Down syndrome having a child. The mother also had Down syndrome. Although the egg was fertilized, the woman had a miscarriage midway through the pregnancy.

Studies have been done on families where either one or both parents had an intellectual disability and a child was born. The studies have shown that these families experienced great difficulties. The parent or parents were unable to cope with the demands and stress of a newborn child. In addition, the child usually suffered from inadequate care because the parents did not know what to do. This was true whether the children in these families were normal or intellectually disabled. Because of such studies, adults with Down syndrome are usually counseled against having children of their own. Instead, they are encouraged to baby-sit for short periods of time or to volunteer in child care centers as substitutes for their parental urge.

Medical Problems

Adults with Down syndrome are susceptible to the same diseases as anyone else who is getting older. But as was the case when growing up, an adult with Down syndrome is more likely to develop certain medical problems than other people are. For example, about 25 percent of adults with Down syndrome develop *Alzheimer's disease,* compared to only 6 percent of the general population. Alzheimer's disease involves changes in the brain that cause people to forget easily, lose their coordination, and become confused. The progress of this disease is often very gradual. A person's condition may not get worse for 10 or even 15 years.

Another medical problem that occurs more often in adults with Down syndrome is seizures. A seizure is sometimes called "a fit" or a convulsion. A seizure occurs when the brain suddenly becomes overactive, resulting in a temporary "short circuit." By the time they are 50 years old, one in ten adults with Down syndrome will have had a seizure. The seizure may be mild or serious.

The most common seizure is called a grand mal seizure. During such a seizure, the person falls to the ground unconscious. At first, the body remains stiff. But then it starts to jerk in a rhythmic pattern for a short period of time. When the seizure is over, the person may fall asleep for a short time before regaining consciousness. Although the person looks as if he or she were suffering during the seizure, it is painless. Medication can be taken to avoid seizures. Like others who have seizures, adults with Down syndrome should wear a bracelet with information about whom to contact in case of an emergency.

Looking Back

Reaching adulthood is no easy task for a child with Down syndrome. The same can be said for their families. As children with Down syndrome reach adulthood, their parents often look back on the years they spent raising them. They realize that the time was filled with mixed emotions. Birth may have been marked by a time of confusion. Infancy may have been a period of protectiveness. The early school years may have brought on concerns. Adolescence may have caused anxiety. Adulthood may have come with pride. These emotions are not unique to families that have a child with Down syndrome. In fact, all families share these emotions as they raise their children. But no doubt, the emotions of a family that has a child with Down syndrome have been more intense.

The Family

IT IS NOW POSSIBLE for a pregnant woman to find out whether her unborn child has Down syndrome. Diagnostic procedures are performed if doctors have some reason to suspect that the unborn child may have Down syndrome. For example, the pregnant woman may be over 40, or she may already have given birth to a child with Down syndrome. Some parents, therefore, may know that their child will be born with Down syndrome. For them, the birth of their child with Down syndrome will come as no surprise. For other parents, it will be a total shock. Although parents react differently to the news that their child has Down syndrome, most will share certain feelings and emotions.

The First Days

The first few days following the birth of a child with Down syndrome are the hardest. Upon learning that their child had Down syndrome, parents have described their feelings as "devastated," "overwhelmed," and "depressed." Some felt as if their world had ended. One couple wrote that when the doctors informed them that their son had Down syndrome, they felt as if "the world opened up and swallowed us right then."

When they hear the words "Down syndrome," parents often feel a sense of shock. They become confused and usually fail to hear what else the doctor is saying. Some parents even faint on hearing the news. Others may have the urge to run away from the whole scene. For many of these parents, what comes to mind on hearing the words "Down syndrome" is an image of a child who is hopelessly retarded.

After the sense of shock has passed, a feeling of disbelief often follows. Anytime a person hears bad news, a natural reaction is to deny it and act as if it never happened. Feeling that there is nothing unusual about the way their child looks, the parents sometimes believe that the doctors have made a mistake. The denial may last for some time—perhaps even for days—as the parents wait for the results of a karyotype the doctor ordered. The test takes several days to complete. As they wait at home with their baby for the results, the parents begin to worry that others might agree with what the doctor has said, so they may not allow anyone, including relatives and friends, to see their child. As an excuse, parents might say that their child is still in the hospital for some minor medical treatment. However, whenever the diagnosis of Down syndrome is confirmed, the sense of denial is shattered.

What usually follows is a sense of deep sorrow. Some parents have compared the sorrow they feel at this point in their lives to a time when their own mother or father had died. In some ways, parents of a child with Down syndrome are feeling the loss of the child they had hoped for and their dreams for that child. Parents may also began to sense that their lives may never be normal—at least for a long time. This realization may make them feel even more sorrow.

Such sadness may lead to anger and bitterness. The parents begin to resent what has happened to them. They become angry about a situation that they cannot change. Rarely is their anger directed toward their baby. Rather, their anger is directed at the world or even at God. Their sorrow and anger are usually expressed by asking how this could possibly have happened to them. They often wind up asking themselves what they did wrong to bring a child with Down syndrome into the world. Thus a feeling of guilt may develop from their sense of anger and bitterness.

Some parents have felt that having a child with Down syndrome is their way of being punished. Mothers especially develop a sense of guilt. After all, they got pregnant, carried the fetus for nine months, and gave birth to the child. They may feel that during all that time they must have done something wrong. Or perhaps it was something they did not do right that resulted in their child being born with Down syndrome. They may fix on some minor incident as being the cause. For example, the mother may think back to the times when she drank a glass of wine with dinner. Perhaps she believes that the alcohol was the cause. Or she may have gained too much weight during her pregnancy. Perhaps she feels that the additional weight was the cause. In any case, many parents search for what they may have done to cause their child to have Down syndrome.

When the karyotype is completed, the parents will eventually know the actual cause. A sense of guilt can really overwhelm the parents at this point. Knowing that Down syndrome is a genetic defect, parents often look to themselves as being responsible. But no one is responsible for his or her genetic makeup or what happens when the genes are sorted as the cells divide. No one has control over which genes are passed on to the next generation. Genes, both good and bad, are always passed from parents to their offspring.

Knowing the reason why their child has Down syndrome may also cause parents to feel inadequate. They may feel that having a child with an inherited disability reflects badly on them. This feeling of inadequacy is usually intensified if the parents have no other children. Parents have said that they felt as if they had let everyone in their family down. Because of this feeling of inadequacy, parents also feel embarrassed. It is not unusual for parents of a newborn with Down syndrome to isolate themselves in their homes. They refuse to allow family and friends to visit their home. When they venture out, their embarrassment may lead them to cover up their child so that the baby is not seen by others.

Embarrassment about their child may lead to rejection of their child. Mothers of a child with Down syndrome have said that they could not even touch their babies for the first day or two while they were in the hospital. And, once home, parents may not give their baby all the care and attention it needs. Then slowly but surely, they begin to see that their baby is as appealing as other babies. The feeling of rejection is gradually replaced by a feeling of acceptance. Eventually *all* the feelings they had those first weeks— shock, disbelief, sorrow, anger, bitterness, guilt, inadequacy, and embarrassment—are usually replaced by the positive feelings that all parents share.

Not all parents, however, can bear the responsibility of raising a child with Down syndrome. Perhaps their child has serious medical problems and requires constant care. Perhaps their child's intelligence is so severely limited that even simple tasks are impossible to do. Perhaps there are too many hardships in the family already for parents to care for a child with Down syndrome. In these cases, parents may have no choice but to place their child in an alternative living arrangement. But for most parents, the process of learning to accept their child begins once their initial reaction and feelings have passed.

Learning to Accept

The first thing the parents usually recognize is that their child is healthier and more alert than they had anticipated. A baby with Down syndrome can have the same happy expression as other babies. Parents see that their child with Down syndrome smiles at the sound of their voices, becomes frightened by loud noises, and cries when he or she is hungry. Parents soon learn that their child is much like others, making it easier for them to accept the situation.

We know that most children with Down syndrome have some degree of mental retardation. Parents are soon told that not all children with Down syndrome are severely

*Babies with Down syndrome bring joy to their families,
along with many challenges.*

retarded and some even have near-normal intelligence. You
have also read about the medical problems these children
face from infancy through adulthood. Parents are soon told
that not all children with Down syndrome have serious
medical problems, and those that do can be treated.
Comforted by this knowledge, parents can begin to cope
with the challenges of bringing up their child.

To begin with, parents must accept the fact that their
child will not grow up intellectually and physically like most
other children. Parents have to realize that their child will
be limited and imperfect. But parents also realize that any
child, even a child without Down syndrome, can be limited
and imperfect. No guarantee exists that a child will grow up
healthy, active, and free of any medical problems. And, no
one can predict what any child will become. All that parents

of a child with Down syndrome can be sure of is that their child will be slower to learn and develop than normal babies. But their child will learn and grow.

Learning to accept their child is easier if the parents are honest about their feelings. Rather than keep their thoughts to themselves, they should talk to others. They should share their frustrations. Sharing their feelings with others is usually more difficult for the fathers of children with Down syndrome. Men sometimes feel that they must "put up a good front" and not show their true feelings. Rather than talk about their sadness and concerns, they often "keep it in."

Talking with others, especially other parents of children with Down syndrome, can help tremendously. Community organizations can help parents locate other families that have a child with Down syndrome. By meeting with these families, parents who have just had a child with Down syndrome will learn that they are not alone in their feelings. These parents will also be able to benefit from the experiences of others. Most of all, they will get the encouragement and hope they need. Seeing what an older child with Down syndrome can accomplish will help them recognize what their child is capable of doing with the proper care and guidance.

Accepting a child with Down syndrome into the family does not mean that the parents must change their lifestyle. In fact, they should gradually return to their normal way of life. Keeping active is a good approach for parents. If possible, involvement in recreational activities and hobbies should be continued. If necessary, parents should arrange for someone to baby-sit their child while they are out of the home. If parents allow their child to disrupt their lives, then they are less likely to accept the child as part of their family.

Parents will also find it easier to accept their child if they do not plan too far ahead. Worrying about their child's education, job prospects, sexuality, and social life should be postponed until the appropriate time. Taking one day at a time is the best way to cope with the arrival of their child. This is especially true with medical concerns. Parents who have a baby with Down syndrome often try to read as much as they can about this condition. Undoubtedly, they will discover all the medical problems that children with Down syndrome can have at various stages in their lives. What these parents need to realize is that many children with Down syndrome are born in good physical health. Parents should not worry about a condition that their child *might* develop.

Accepting a child with Down syndrome also means that the parents will show off their baby like any other parents. Most relatives and friends feel uncomfortable and do not know how to respond when they first see the child. They may have misconceptions about Down syndrome. To be sure that their child is accepted by others, parents will have to educate their relatives and friends about Down syndrome. Nonetheless, some people express their sorrow upon learning that the baby has Down syndrome, and they may even offer sympathy to the parents. The parents should realize that these people are trying to be kind in their own way. To prove that sympathy is not needed, all the parents need do is show everyone how their baby has been accepted into their family.

Sibling Response

The arrival of a baby always causes changes in a family, especially if there are other children. Siblings look forward to the arrival of their new brother or sister, and the arrival of a baby with Down syndrome is no different. Most children respond well to being the brother or sister of a child with Down syndrome. In fact, older siblings are often more considerate and caring toward a younger brother or sister with Down syndrome than they would be toward a normal child. Such feelings of concern can develop even if the baby with Down syndrome is placed in a health care facility and never brought home. Siblings have been known to identify with their brother or sister with Down syndrome even if he or she does not live at home. Parents have told of cases where their children have felt sad and guilty about a brother or sister who never became part of the family.

The ages of the siblings affect how well they accept a younger brother or sister with Down syndrome. An older sibling will be more mature and thus more likely to be accepting. But, no matter what their age, all siblings need to understand what Down syndrome is and have some idea of how it will affect their younger brother or sister. Children under the age of three are too young to understand anything about Down syndrome, of course. Basically these children will imitate how their parents act toward the baby with Down syndrome. If the parents act with love and care, then a sibling under three years of age will do the same. If the parents fail to accept the child with Down syndrome, then the sibling will probably have a negative attitude.

After the age of three, siblings can begin to understand what Down syndrome means. The older the sibling is, the

Siblings are usually quick to accept a younger brother or sister with Down syndrome.

more details he or she can be given. Any sibling just over three years old needs to know only that Down syndrome is a disability. The sibling should also be aware that the disability will affect how their brother or sister will grow intellectually and physically. Any sibling more than 12 years old can be told the details about the causes and consequences of Down syndrome.

Acceptance by siblings does not mean that they will not be jealous at times. All brothers and sisters are jealous of one another at various times when growing up. Sibling rivalry happens in all families, including those that have a child with Down syndrome. Parents must be careful not to spoil the child with Down syndrome. They should not, for example, favor the child with more toys or extra attention. Any favored treatment by parents creates even more jealousy on the part of siblings toward the brother or sister with Down syndrome. The child with Down syndrome should become part of the usual household routine but should never be made the focus of family life.

Some parents try to prevent jealousy from arising by setting aside special days just for their nondisabled children. The parents let these children plan the family activities for the special day. If these plans involve leaving the house, the parents get a sitter to care for the baby with Down syndrome. If the parents are reluctant to leave their baby with a sitter, they may use a respite care service. This service provides relief for parents on either a short- or long-term basis. In some cases, trained aides are available to come to the home to provide care for the baby while the rest of the family is out. In addition, there are day care respites run by a group of parents who volunteer on a rotating basis. A traditional day care center may also be available for families who wish to enjoy a special day. With such respite services available, families have been able to set aside special days on a regular basis for years. And being provided with these special days has made it easier for some siblings to accept their brother or sister with Down syndrome.

Even if siblings have no problem accepting their brother or sister with Down syndrome, they may be upset by comments that their friends make. Being the brother or sister of a child with Down syndrome makes siblings the targets of unkind comments and teasing by others. Siblings have to develop a way of coping with this situation, and parents need to recognize that they must be available to listen. They must allow their children to express their anger and resentment, just as they themselves must be open about their feelings. If siblings are not allowed to express their feelings about the situation, then they may come to resent their brother or sister with Down syndrome.

Parents can also look for help in other ways. Several books have been written for siblings of children with a disability such as Down syndrome. These books tell of the frustrations and anger felt by siblings as they grew up with their disabled brother or sister. In addition, parents can have their children become part of a sibling support group. Like the groups designed for parents, these groups give siblings the opportunity to share their feelings and their experiences. The groups are supervised by a trained professional. In many cases, siblings find it easier to talk about their feelings with their peers than with their parents.

Early Intervention

One of the first things parents of a child with Down syndrome must do is seek early intervention. Early intervention means that parents begin working with their baby early on so that he or she develops to the fullest extent possible. Early intervention can take many forms, depending on the needs of each baby with Down syndrome. In every case, however, a program is developed that consists of a plan of specific and specialized ways to promote the baby's development. As the baby grows and develops, the program is changed accordingly.

Early intervention requires professional help. Professionals who might be called upon to help include doctors, nurses, teachers, and therapists who have had experience in dealing with Down syndrome babies. Each professional has a different speciality and serves a different function.

A speech therapist works patiently to help this child use oral and facial muscles to make sounds.

For example, a speech therapist teaches the Down syndrome baby how to use the muscles of his or her mouth and face to eat and make sounds. Other therapists work with the parents to teach the baby such skills as reaching for a bottle, grabbing a pacifier, or shaking a rattle. Doctors and nurses assist the parents with daily medications and with the use of any necessary equipment such as feeding tubes and sleep apnea monitors. Teachers focus on the baby's intellectual and social development. They begin by working to develop the child's responses to stimulation. For example, they try to get the child to follow the movement of objects with his or her eyes.

An early intervention program not only helps the child with Down syndrome develop, it also provides support for the family. Parents and siblings are taught specific techniques to use in developing the Down syndrome child's intellectual and physical skills. In addition, the professionals in an early intervention program support the parents and siblings in their efforts to make the child part of the family. Finally, the program gives parents the skills and attitude needed to deal with problems that might arise as the baby passes through infancy, the early school years, adolescence, and adulthood. The family will probably face some type of problem as their child with Down syndrome grows up. But the future will hopefully provide a solution to some of these problems.

CHAPTER 9

The Future

Since Dr. Langdon Down first described the traits common to children with Down syndrome in 1866, significant advances have been made in the medical procedures and treatments available. Various care and support services are now offered for parents who are raising a child with Down syndrome. In addition, early intervention and inclusion programs are designed to help children with Down syndrome reach their maximum potential. But despite all these steps, one major hurdle has not been overcome. Down syndrome is still a condition that cannot be cured.

False Hopes

Like any incurable disease or condition, Down syndrome has been a target for those looking for a "magic bullet" that will prove to be an effective cure. Over the years, several "cures" for Down syndrome have been promoted. Many parents, desperately wishing their child to be like most other children, have become involved with programs that claim they can cure Down syndrome. Some programs do not promise a cure, but claim that they can greatly improve the way a child with Down syndrome develops.

Programs that promote either a cure or a significant improvement have so far produced only false hopes. In addition, these programs can be quite expensive, putting an additional financial burden on a family that may already have considerable medical expenses. But the real danger of these programs is that they may actually harm the intellectual, physical, and psychological growth of the child.

Diets

Most of the programs that claim to bring about significant improvements involve special diets. Various diets have been recommended for children with Down syndrome. One includes giving them huge doses of vitamins and minerals. Hair samples from the child with Down syndrome are analyzed to develop a profile of what vitamins and minerals are considered to be deficient. The child is then given large doses of those vitamins and minerals. But the level that is considered deficient in these children would usually be considered acceptable by most people, including doctors. So these children actually wind up having very high levels of vitamins and minerals in their bodies. You may think that these high levels would benefit the body and make it able to function more efficiently. After all, if vitamins and minerals are good for you, then more should be better. However, the opposite is sometimes true.

Certain vitamins, like vitamin C and B complex, dissolve in water. Such vitamins are said to be water-soluble. If too much vitamin C is present in the body, the excess amount collects in the part of the blood called the *plasma*. Plasma is the liquid part of the blood that consists mostly of water. The excess vitamins are transported in the plasma to the kidneys and excreted in the urine. In order to excrete these excess vitamins, the kidneys have to "work overtime." Over a long period of time, the kidneys may become damaged from "overwork."

A more immediate threat is posed by vitamins that cannot dissolve in water but can dissolve in fats. Such vitamins, like vitamins A and D, are said to be fat-soluble. The fats that contain excess vitamins cannot be excreted in the urine but instead collect in the liver. As a result, fatty deposits may develop in the liver. As the largest organ in the body, the liver performs many functions. One of the liver's jobs is to destroy any toxic chemicals, such as alcohol, that may be present in the blood. Fatty deposits interfere with the liver's work. So, taking high doses of fat-soluble vitamins over a long period of time may cause liver damage. In turn, liver damage can lead to serious illness and even death.

Other diets have also been recommended for children with Down syndrome. These include diets that recommend avoiding foods to which the child is allergic and foods to which certain artificial coloring agents have been added. Some children with Down syndrome have been noted to be less hyperactive and more focused after being on a diet that avoids such foods. Any improvement in behavior, however, is only slight. In fact, a child without Down syndrome on the same type of diet shows the same improvement in behavior. Scientific studies have yet to show that any diet is effective in bringing about a significant improvement in children with Down syndrome.

Therapies

A recent finding in the treatment of *Parkinson's disease* has provided some people with support in their belief that a similar procedure works in the case of Down syndrome. Parkinson's disease is a disorder involving a deficiency in dopamine, a chemical substance that the brain requires to function normally. Without this chemical, the brain causes parts of the body, such as the hands, to shake uncontrollably. A recent experimental approach involves injecting human brain cells into the brain of a person with Parkinson's disease. In some cases, there have been dramatic improvements in people who have been injected with these brain cells.

A similar procedure has been used in trying to cure Down syndrome. This procedure involves injecting brain cells from lamb and calf fetuses into children with Down syndrome. This process is usually repeated each month over a five- to six-month period. Supporters of this procedure have claimed that it improves the child's general development, including growth in height and weight. However, scientific studies have shown no improvement in children who have received this therapy. In addition, the risks of this treatment have not yet been established.

Another therapy promoted by some people as a cure for Down syndrome is known as patterning. Patterning is intensive, time-consuming, and expensive. Several trained people work with the child's head and limbs in specific patterns or routines. The process can take all day. The idea is that the brain will recognize and respond to these patterns by reorganizing itself. However, no scientific evidence exists to show that patterning has brought any significant improvement in children with Down syndrome.

Other attempts have been made either to cure Down syndrome or to bring about some significant improvement in the condition. These attempts have included various medicines, *chiropractors* who manipulate the child's spine, and the use of eye exercises to promote brain function. None have shown any promise. With all these failures, you might think that the future is bleak for children with Down syndrome, but something is happening right now that may prove to be a truly significant development in the story of Down syndrome.

The Human Genome Project

Down syndrome is an inherited condition. Because about 95 percent of individuals with Down syndrome have an extra chromosome 21, scientists working on Down syndrome have a great interest in this chromosome. Specifically, they would like to know how an extra copy of this chromosome can bring about the many physical changes that occur in Down syndrome. Because chromosomes contain the genes that control an individual's physical development, the researchers first have to determine what genes are on chromosome 21. Their work is part of a larger project known as the Human Genome Project.

Started in 1990, the Human Genome Project is an international effort that will cost billions of dollars. Scientists throughout the world are working to identify the location of all the genes on the 23 pairs of chromosomes in humans.

Human chromosomes contain an estimated 80,000 genes. But it is not just the number of genes that make the Human Genome Project so difficult, it is also the gene's chemical nature. A gene is made of a chemical compound called *deoxyribonucleic acid (DNA)*. A *genome* is all the DNA in the cell of an organism. Thus scientists involved in the Human Genome Project are trying to unravel the basic structure of all the DNA in human chromosomes.

DNA is made up of four similar chemicals called bases that are abbreviated with the letters A, T, G, and C. These bases exist as pairs within the DNA. A base pair consists of either G-C or A-T. Scientists estimate that 3 billion base pairs make up the 80,000 genes, which in turn make up the 23 pairs of chromosomes. In effect, the scientists working on the Human Genome Project must determine the specific order in which the As, Ts, Gs, and Cs are arranged in the base pairs that make up the genes on the chromosomes.

Using sophisticated techniques, scientists have determined the sequence of base pairs in the DNA of several simple organisms. For example, they know the sequence of bases in the DNA of various viruses and bacteria. But the DNAs of viruses and bacteria are far simpler in structure than those of humans, so the challenge in sequencing the DNA of humans is much greater.

In the first seven years of the Human Genome Project, only 1 percent of the human genome had been sequenced. At this rate, it would take scientists hundreds of years to finish the job. Fortunately, new techniques are constantly being developed by scientists to speed up the process. By 1998, 2.7 percent of the human genome had been sequenced. In just one year, scientists had almost tripled the rate at which they can sequence the human genome. Hopefully, each year will bring progressively faster techniques.

The Human Genome Project may enable scientists to identify the gene or genes on chromosome 21 responsible for Down syndrome. Their work may also lead them to understand why these genes, if they exist, operate only when they are present in more than the usual number— when there are three copies of chromosome 21 rather than two. If they are successful in identifying such genes, the logical next step would be to develop methods of removing these genes before they have had a chance to function.

A second possibility is that scientists may discover that Down syndrome is not caused by the presence of extra genes. Instead, Down syndrome may be the result of a gene or genes that are defective in some way. Scientists can determine if this is the case by comparing the sequence of bases in the DNA of individuals with Down syndrome to those of normal people. Their job would then be to find a way of correcting the defect in the gene or genes.

A third possibility is that scientists may discover individuals with Down syndrome lack a specific gene or genes. In this case, their job would be to develop methods to insert the needed gene or genes into the DNA of individuals with Down syndrome. The process of removing, correcting, or inserting a gene is known as *gene therapy*. Gene therapy may prove to be a way to cure not only Down syndrome but also a number of other inherited conditions.

Animal Models

Scientists try whenever possible to use animals for their studies of human diseases. Obviously, scientists cannot experiment with humans. A suitable alternative would be an animal that could serve as a model of what might happen in humans under various experimental conditions. Laboratory mice have been used quite successfully as models to study Down syndrome.

One of the first laboratory mice to be studied in relation to Down syn-

Laboratory mice have been used as models by scientists studying Down syndrome.

drome was the "trisomy 16" mouse. As the names implies, these mice were deliberately altered so that their cells would contain three copies of their chromosome number 16. Like humans with Down syndrome, these mice live to adulthood but develop learning problems.

Recently, scientists have been able to transplant parts of human chromosome 21 into laboratory mice. In 1997, their work led to the first report of a link between a specific gene on chromosome 21 and mental retardation. This is the first reported success of pinpointing the gene on chromosome 21 that might be responsible for Down syndrome. Scientists named this gene DYRK, letters that represent the protein it produces. Scientists suspect that this protein interferes with the development of pathways in the brain that are essential to learning. Since DYRK was first identified, scientists now suspect that between 20 and 40 genes may play a role in Down syndrome. But no gene has yet been positively linked to any feature associated with this condition.

Future Protection

Despite its promises, the Human Genome Project has raised concerns among some people. These people fear that the knowledge gained from the project may not be in the best interests of many people. Their concern centers on the fact that scientists will probably discover the genes responsible for a variety of diseases. Laboratory tests now exist to determine if a person has a gene for certain diseases, and more such tests will be developed in the future as the location and makeup of more and more genes become known.

Health and life insurance companies may require a person to take these tests before they issue a policy. If a person has a gene for a particular disease, then he or she may have to pay more than someone else for the same insurance coverage. And a person who has a gene for a more serious or life-threatening disease may be denied insurance coverage. In this case, insurance companies can say that medical expenses will probably be too high for them to absorb.

What may happen in the future to many people who want health insurance is already a reality today for adults with Down syndrome. An individual with Down syndrome already faces an uncertain future with respect to health insurance. As you can imagine, having Down syndrome can result in major medical bills. Hospital costs for open-heart surgery alone can run into the tens of thousands of dollars. Costs for therapists who are needed on a regular basis can quickly mount up. Even if nothing is medically wrong with the child, visits to doctors' offices for comprehensive physical exams can be expensive. Unfortunately, most insurance companies do not offer health insurance at a reasonable price to children or adults with Down syndrome. In fact, many do not offer health insurance at any price.

Many children with Down syndrome are covered under their family's health insurance policy. However, this coverage usually ends when the child reaches 19 years of age or a little later if he or she attends college. As an adult, a person with Down syndrome may face the possibility of paying a very high price for health insurance or perhaps being unable to get any coverage at all.

About half the states in the U.S. have passed laws that prohibit insurance companies from denying health coverage because of a disability like Down syndrome. However, these laws have loopholes that allow companies to deny health insurance to someone with a disability. Thus these laws are ineffective. They do not accomplish what they were supposed to do. Some states have recognized that these laws are ineffective and have taken steps to correct them. In some cases, they have passed laws that make it illegal to deny health insurance coverage to a person with a disability for any reason whatsoever. Other states have established "assigned risk pools." These "pools" consist of people with various disabilities, including Down syndrome. The medical expenses for the people in such a "pool" are shared among all the insurance companies in the state.

Planning for the Future

There are many problems and concerns that parents of a child with Down syndrome may encounter. Not all these parents face the same medical problems or have to deal with the same social difficulties while their child is growing up. But there is one concern that all these parents do share. They want to be sure that their child is prepared for the time when they will not be around to provide care and support. As one parent put it, "We want Josh to grow into a person who can function on his own, with a little structure here and there. We want him to help take care of himself. There may come a day when he has to fend for himself. We want him to be able to do that."

Myths and Truths

MOST PEOPLE have not read anything about Down syndrome. Without having the facts, their beliefs and opinions about Down syndrome are based more on hearsay than anything else. Misconceptions about Down syndrome have been common ever since 1866 when Dr. Langdon Down described children with this condition. Since that time, the general public has come to accept a number of myths about Down syndrome.

Myth: Down syndrome is a very rare condition.
Truth: Approximately 1 in 1,000 live births results in a child with Down syndrome. In the United States alone, about 5,500 babies are born each year with Down syndrome. Today, about 250,000 individuals in the Unites States and

millions of people throughout the world have Down syndrome.

Myth: Down syndrome affects only certain groups of people.
Truth: Down syndrome can affect anyone regardless of their race, religion, nationality, wealth, or social status.

Myth: Down syndrome may not appear or be evident until later in life.
Truth: As an inherited condition, Down syndrome is evident at birth. A baby with this condition will possess a number of features that are characteristic of Down syndrome. In fact, the presence of these features at birth will make a doctor suspect that the child has Down syndrome.

Myth: There is no way of knowing whether a child will be born with Down syndrome.
Truth: Two procedures—amniocentensis and chorionic villus sampling—are available to pregnant women who want to know if their unborn child has Down syndrome. Both procedures involve the preparation of a karyotype that will definitely reveal whether the fetus has Down syndrome. In addition, several screening tests are available that can be used to indicate whether the unborn child has Down syndrome. These screening tests are not definitive, but a positive result is often followed up with either amniocentesis or chorionic villus sampling.

Myth: Most children with Down syndrome are born to older parents.
Truth: As a woman gets older, her chances of having a child with Down syndrome increase. However, nearly 80 percent

of children with Down syndrome are born to mothers younger than 35.

Myth: Although Down syndrome is inherited, its exact cause is not known.

Truth: Down syndrome has three genetic scenarios. About 95 percent of individuals with Down syndrome have trisomy 21, or three copies of chromosome 21. The extra copy is usually inherited from the mother. The remaining 5 percent of individuals with Down syndrome are divided between those that have a chromosomal translocation and those that are the result of mosaicism.

Myth: Babies with Down syndrome tend to be fatter than other babies.

Truth: Babies with Down syndrome tend to weigh less and be shorter than other babies. This is due to their difficulty in swallowing and eating and their genetic condition which leads to short stature.

Myth: All children with Down syndrome look and act alike.

Truth: Children with Down syndrome share certain physical features that characterize the condition and make them easily recognizable. These include the facial features that Dr. Down first described in 1866. However, just like other children, no two children with Down syndrome are exactly alike. Each child with Down syndrome displays the same wide range of personality traits as other children. Like any other child, a child with Down syndrome is unique.

Myth: All children with Down syndrome have severe mental retardation.

A high school diploma is the beginning of a successful life for this young man.

Truth: Some children with Down syndrome are severely retarded with IQs below 40. However, most children with Down syndrome have IQs between 40 and 70 and thus have only moderate to mild mental retardation. Some have IQs that place them in the near-normal range of intelligence. Caution is advised in evaluating a Down syndrome child's intelligence on the basis of IQ tests. The child may have the knowledge but be unable to express it fully because of some physical difficulty or medical problem. Thus an IQ score may not truly reflect the skills and abilities of a child with Down syndrome.

Myth: Because of their mental retardation, children with Down syndrome cannot learn.
Truth: All children with Down syndrome can—and do—learn. Their learning process is just slower. Children with Down syndrome are no different than those who have mental retardation because of some other condition.

Myth: Children with Down syndrome usually die young.

Truth: In the early 1900s, the average life expectancy for a child with Down syndrome was 9 years. By the mid-1900s, this figure increased to 40 years. Today, 80 percent of individuals with Down syndrome live to at least age 55.

Myth: Most children with Down syndrome are placed in institutions.

Truth: This was the case in the early 1900s. Placed in institutions, children with Down syndrome were given little medical care and no intellectual stimulation. Thus, their life expectancy was short. Today, most children with Down syndrome are taken care of at home, often with community assistance. The exceptions are those children who have severe mental retardation and multiple physical disabilities. Because these children need more care than can usually be provided at home, they are often placed in institutions where such care is available.

Myth: Little community support is available to families of a child with Down syndrome.

Truth: Beginning in the 1960s, a number of support services became available to families of children with Down syndrome. These services came about because of concerns expressed by parents of children with Down syndrome and other disabilities. These parents felt that their children should have the same opportunities as others. To support them in their efforts, community organizations have developed various programs. These programs range from providing group homes where adults with Down syndrome can live to offering respite services that allow families to take breaks from the demands of raising a child with Down syndrome. Today, nearly every community in the country has parent-support groups.

Myth: Little national support is available to families of a child with Down syndrome.

Truth: There are several national organizations that provide support and information to families of a child with Down syndrome (see Resources). In addition, many states have local chapters of these national organizations. Some of these organizations deal only with Down syndrome, while others are concerned with issues involving children with any disability. The federal government has also become actively involved in addressing issues dealing with individuals with disabilities. Congress has passed several laws, including the Rehabilitation Act in 1973, the Individuals with Disabilities Education Act in 1975, and the Americans with Disabilities Act in 1990. These laws are designed to provide equal opportunities in education, housing, recreation, and employment to people with disabilities, including Down syndrome.

Myth: Children with Down syndrome must be placed in education programs that are segregated from the rest of the school.

Truth: As a result of the policy of "inclusion," children with Down syndrome are part of the regular education program in schools throughout the United States. The extent to which they are included depends on each child's Individualized Education Plan (IEP). While some children with Down syndrome are included in the regular classroom for all subjects, most children with this condition are involved in regular classes on a more limited basis.

Myth: Children with Down syndrome are always happy and smiling.

Truth: The facial features associated with Down syndrome may give people the false impression that these children are always carefree and happy. But children with Down syndrome have the same feelings as everyone else. They are happy and smiling when they feel accepted. They are sad and upset when they are treated badly.

Myth: Children with Down syndrome do not grow up physically in the same way as other children.

Truth: Children with Down syndrome are more likely than other children to have medical problems. These problems often begin at birth and can slow down their development. For example, a child normally begins walking at about 13 months of age, while a child with Down syndrome starts to walk at about 24 months of age. Medical problems may continue to trouble them as they grow older, delaying their physical growth. But children with Down syndrome will eventually grow up physically.

Myth: Children with Down syndrome have medical problems that cannot be treated.

Truth: Because of the advances made in both diagnosis and treatment, medical conditions associated with Down syndrome can be corrected. The most notable advances have been made in open-heart surgery to repair holes that allow the blood to mix. In the past, it was not possible to perform such surgery on small infants, but surgeons now have the skills, knowledge, and support systems to do it. The ability to diagnose a condition sooner makes it more likely that the treatment will be effective. Procedures such as echocardiograms and electrocardiograms have made it possible for doctors to detect a heart defect before any serious or permanent damage is done.

Myth: Children with Down syndrome do not develop sexually.

Truth: Children with Down syndrome pass through the same sequence of changes during puberty as other adolescents. Hormone levels in boys rise, causing their voices to change and enabling their testes to produce sperm. Hormone levels also rise in girls, causing their breasts to enlarge and initiating their menstrual cycles. Adults with Down syndrome are sexually mature and can marry and have children. Some women with Down syndrome have become mothers.

Myth: Any child born to a woman with Down syndrome will also have Down syndrome.

Truth: A woman with Down syndrome may or may not have a child with the same condition depending on what caused the woman herself to have Down syndrome. If she has trisomy 21, there is a 50 percent chance that her child will have Down syndrome and a 50 percent chance that her child will be normal. The chances are different if the Down syndrome was caused by a translocation or mosaicism. In any case, a married woman with Down syndrome should speak with a doctor about her chances of having a child with the same condition.

Myth: Adults with Down syndrome cannot be employed.

Truth: Many adults with Down syndrome are successfully employed. Some have jobs in the regular work world as cashiers, clerks, messengers, short-order cooks, and laborers. Others are employed in sheltered work environments that do not have the demands and stress of the regular work world. Here adults with Down syndrome work with other disabled people in a structured and supervised environment.

Myth: A "mongoloid idiot" is a term that can be applied to a person with Down syndrome.

Truth: Dr. Down attempted to find a connection between intelligence and race. He felt that because of their facial features, individuals with Down syndrome were part of a race of Asian people known as Mongols. Their mental retardation led Dr. Down to classify them as "idiots." Today, the term "mongoloid idiot" is obsolete and should never be used. Down syndrome has no relationship to any race, religion, or nationality. In addition, most people with Down syndrome have only mild to moderate mental retardation and thus cannot be classified as "idiots."

Myth: An individual with Down syndrome will never be able to lead an independent life.

Truth: Many adults with Down syndrome have developed the maturity and skills to move out of their homes. Rarely, however, do they live completely on their own. They usually live in group homes or residences with others who have some disability. In a group-home setting, trained professionals are available to provide help when needed, but the daily chores are often the responsibility of the residents.

Assisted by a guide, this young woman experiences the thrill of rock climbing.

Myth: Individuals with Down syndrome are limited as to what they can physically do.

Truth: Many individuals with Down syndrome are physically limited to some extent, primarily because of their low muscle tone or a problem with the vertebrae in their neck. But if a child has no vertebrae problem, then the American Academy of Pediatrics Association recommends that he or she be included in all gym activities in school.

Myth: Unlike the situation with other health problems such as cancer and AIDS, little or no research is being done on Down syndrome.

Truth: Scientists are working to develop a "genetic map" for chromosome 21. They hope to identify the genetic basis of

Down syndrome. If they can pinpoint the location of the gene or genes responsible for Down syndrome, gene therapy may lead to a cure.

Myth: There is no cure for Down syndrome.
Truth: In this case, unfortunately, the myth is also the truth. There is no cure for Down syndrome—yet.

A Note on Sources

THE FOLLOWING BOOKS were used for factual information and anecdotal stories about children with Down syndrome.

Berube, Michael. *Life As We Know It: A Father, a Family, and an Exceptional Child.* New York: Random House, 1996.

McClurg, Eunice. *Your Down Syndrome Child.* New York: Doubleday and Co., 1986.

Selikowitz, Mark. *Down Syndrome: The Facts.* New York: Oxford University Press, 1997.

Stray-Gundersen, Karen, ed. *Babies with Down Syndrome.* Bethesda, MD: Woodbine House, 1995.

Glossary

adenoid—a small mass of cells in the back of the throat

Alzheimer's disease—a disease that causes changes in the brain that result in loss of memory and coordination

amniocentesis—a procedure used to determine the karyotype of a fetus by removing cells from the fluid that surrounds the fetus. It also detects other genetic problems.

astigmatism—blurred vision caused by an irregularly shaped cornea

atria (singular, atrium)—upper chamber of the heart

atrioventricular septal defect—a hole in the muscle wall that separates the two sides of the heart

bronchitis—inflammation of the tubes leading from the trachea to the lungs

cell—the basic unit that makes up the structure of the body

chiropractor—a person who treats illnesses by adjusting the spine

chorionic villi sampling (CVS)—procedure used to determine the karyotype of a fetus by removing cells from a structure used to nourish the fetus. It detects other genetic problems, as well.

chromosome—a rod-shaped structure inside the cell on which the genes are located

congenital defect—disorder that is present at birth

daughter cell—cell produced by mitosis

deoxyribonucleic acid (DNA)—chemical that makes up a gene on the chromosome

disjunction—separation of the members of a chromosome pair during cell division

Down syndrome—abnormal condition marked by some degree of mental retardation and certain distinct physical features

epicanthic fold—small fold of skin at the corners of each eye of a child with Down syndrome

esophagus—food passage leading to the stomach

estrogen—female sex hormone

eustachian tube—narrow passageway that leads from the middle ear to the throat

fetus—unborn baby

gene—basic unit of heredity that is present on a chromosome

gene therapy—procedure used to insert or delete a gene from a chromosome or to correct a defective gene

genetics—study of heredity, or how traits are passed from parents to their offspring

genome—all the DNA in a cell or an organism

hormone—chemical substance that is produced by a gland and travels in the bloodstream

hypothyroidism—condition in which the thyroid gland is underactive and tends to get larger

karyotype—arrangement showing all the chromosomes in an individual

leukemia—cancer of the white blood cells

meiosis—process by which mature sperm and eggs are produced in preparation for fertilization

menstruation—cycle in which a female produces a mature egg cell; commonly referred to as a "period"

metabolism—all the chemical processes that occur in the body, such as digestion and respiration

miscarriage—spontaneous end of a pregnancy

mitosis—process by which a parent cell divides to produce two daughter cells

mosaicism—condition in which the cells of an individual have different numbers of chromosomes

muscle tone—normal tension, or responsiveness to stimuli (such as stretching)

nondisjunction—failure of the members of a chromosome pair to separate properly during a cell division

orthopedic—relating to the bones

ovary—female sex organ

parent cell—cell that undergoes cell division

Parkinson's disease—brain disorder that results in uncontrolled movements of certain parts of the body

pituitary gland—gland located at the base of the brain that controls many other glands, including those involved in sexual maturation

plasma—liquid part of the blood consisting mostly of water

pneumonia—infection of the lungs

protein—chemical compound that is made under the control of a gene

puberty—the time when a person's body changes from a child's to an adult's

Punnett square—a grid used to determine the odds of a particular event occurring as a result of fertilization

sex chromosomes—a pair of chromosomes that determines the sex of an individual

sex hormones—hormones responsible for the development of reproductive maturity

sleep apnea—temporary stoppage of breathing during sleep

strabismus—imbalance in the muscles of the eye so that they cross and cannot focus properly

syndrome—collection of features or symptoms that characterize or indicate a disease or some abnormal condition

testes (singular, testis)—male sex organ

testosterone—male sex hormone

thyroid gland—structure in the neck that produces a hormone

thyroxin—hormone that controls metabolism, produced by the thyroid gland

trachea—air passageway leading to the lungs

translocation—transfer of a piece of chromosome from one chromosome to another

trisomy—presence of three chromosomes instead of the normal pair

trisomy 21—another term for Down syndrome; the presence of three copies of chromosome 21

valve—flap between the chambers of the heart that keeps blood flowing in the correct direction

ventricle—lower chamber of the heart

vertebrae—bones that make up the spinal cord or backbone

Further Readings

Berube, Michael. *Life As We Know It: A Father, a Family, and an Exceptional Child.* New York: Random House, 1996.

Dolce, Laura. *Mental Retardation.* Broomall, PA: Chelsea House, 1994.

Garcia, Ann. *Down Syndrome.* Denver, CO: Baker-Hill Publishing, 1995.

Hassold, Terry J. *Down Syndrome: A Promising Future, Together.* New York: John Wiley and Sons, 1998.

Levitz, Mitchell. *Count Us In: Growing Up with Down Syndrome.* San Diego, CA: Harvest Books, 1994.

Resources

National Organizations
and Web Sites

Association for Children with Down Syndrome
2616 Martin Avenue
Bellemore, NY 11710-3196
516-221-4700
E-mail: info@acds.org
http://www.acds.org

This association is a national organization that provides books, articles, and videos dealing with Down syndrome.

March of Dimes Birth Defects Foundation
1275 Mamaroneck Avenue
White Plains, NY 10605
http://www.modimes.org

This organization deals with any disability a newborn baby might have, including Down syndrome.

National Association for Down Syndrome
P.O. Box 4542
Oak Brook, IL 60522-4542
http://www.nads.org

This association is a national organization that provides information about Down syndrome and has educational videos and pamphlets.

National Down Syndrome Congress (NDSC)
1605 Chantilly Drive
Suite 250
Atlanta, GA 30324-3269
800-232-6372
E-mail: ndsc@charitiesusa.com
http://www.carol.net/~ndsc

The NDSC is a national organization of parents and professionals. They publish two newsletters by and for people with Down syndrome: "Down Syndrome News" and "Down Syndrome Health News." They also publish information sheets and booklets for the general public.

National Down Syndrome Society (NDSS)
666 Broadway
New York, NY 10012
800-221-4602
212-979-2873 (FAX)
http://www.ndss.org

The NDSS is a national organization that seeks to promote a better understanding of Down syndrome. The organization publishes "News and Views" for people with Down syndrome, and information sheets and booklets for the general public.

Pathfinder Village

http://www.pathfindervillage.org

This site contains an extensive list of sites that deal with Down syndrome. Included are sites of organizations in individual states, online magazines and newsletters, medical resources, international pages, and individual and family pages.

Index

Italics indicate pages
with illustrations

About the Author

AFTER TEACHING high school biology and chemistry for twenty-five years, Salvatore Tocci now devotes his working time to writing science books. Since his retirement, Mr. Tocci has written seven books and has served as senior author on the revision of a high school textbook that focuses on the practical applications of chemistry. A resident of East Hampton, New York, he spends his spare time during the winter months working in his darkroom and constructing his 12 x 24 HO train layout. During the warmer times of the year, he and his wife Patti spend time on their sailboat, the *Royal T.*